DR. RUTH
WESTHEIMER

Margaret M. Scariano

—Contemporary Women Series—

ENSLOW PUBLISHERS, INC.

Bloy St. and Ramsey Ave.   P.O. Box 38
Box 777   Aldershot
Hillside, N.J. 07205   Hants GU12 6BP
U.S.A.   U.K.

Library of Congress Cataloging-in-Publication Data

Scariano, Margaret M.
    Dr. Ruth Westheimer/Margaret M. Scariano.
      p.   cm.— (Contemporary women series)
    Includes bibliographical references (p.   ) and index.
    Summary: Traces the life of well-known sex therapist Dr. Ruth
Westheimer, from her early childhood in Nazi Germany through her
life in America to her success as a radio and television
personality.
    ISBN 0-89490-333-0
      1. Westheimer, Ruth K. (Ruth Karola), 1928– —Juvenile
literature. 2. Sex therapists—United States—Biography—Juvenile
literature. [1. Westheimer, Ruth K. (Ruth Karola), 1928– .
2. Sex therapists.] I. Title. II. Series.
RC438.6.W47S25   1992
616.85'83'0092—dc20
[B]   91-40923
                                             CIP
                                           AC

Printed in the United States of America

10 9 8 7 6 5 4 3 2 1

Illustration Credits: AP/Wide World Photos, pp. 8, 18, 28, 30, 31, 38, 65, 73,
76, 81, 82, 88, 99, 103, 104, 110, 113; Raeanne Rubenstein, pp. 96, 112, 117.

Cover Photo: Globe Photos, Inc.

Dedicated to
Marion, Linda, Susan, Kelly, and Bill

Contents

Foreword

After reading *Dr. Ruth Westheimer*, I realized how similar my life was to other children's. I, too, had loving parents and grandparents. Like any child I liked special treats and special holidays and special friends. And yet, my life has been different because of the events of history.

In this book, Margaret M. Scariano has highlighted the experiences that helped shape my life and motivated me to get an education. Young people will be fascinated by the historical events that led to my being one of the Kinder Transport children who were fortunate in escaping the horrors of Hitler's Germany. I've enjoyed reading this book and remembering both the happy and sad times that led to my becoming "Dr. Ruth." I'm sure that you too will enjoy it.

Ruth K.
Westheimer

Dr. Ruth Westheimer

1

An Audience With Dr. Ruth

The theme music fades and the camera moves in on a small woman in a bright floral dress. The studio audience applauds and the camera focuses on the roomful of teenagers. With microphone in hand, the ash-blond woman walks briskly toward the young people.

In a high-pitched voice flavored with a strong European accent, she welcomes her studio guests with a pixielike smile and tells them they are going to talk about friendships, what makes friendships work and what destroys them. She urges her guests to tell how they feel about the good things or not so good things in their friendships. Every eye is on the four-foot, seven-inch tall woman as she bounces, microphone in hand, from one individual to the next. Questioning. Listening. Talking.

Who is this bundle of energy and enthusiasm? None other than the dynamic Dr. Ruth Westheimer—wife, mother, author, psychotherapist, family and sex counselor, and radio and television personality.

And it is this strong personality that reaches out to people and draws them out. On her Lifetime cable show, she jumps right in with questions.

"Who has a best friend?" she asks.

A few hands go up. Dr. Ruth nods to a young girl in the second row.

"I used to have a best friend and she used me for a lot of stuff—like money and anything [else] she could get her hands on." The girl smiles, but there is a tremor in her voice.

"And what happened? She was your best friend and . . ." Dr. Ruth moves across the room. She seems to be in motion at all times.

"She would leave me and go with other people and spend my money on them." The young girl's voice fades.

"I hope you rrrrealize she was not a best friend." Dr. Ruth says, her r's reverberating. "Did you find another friend?"

"Yes."

"Terrrrific." Dr. Ruth answers, the r's rolling off her tongue like marbles. "Anyone else?"

More hands go up and Dr. Ruth walks quickly to the other side of the room. She pauses in front of a dark-haired girl. "You had a best friend? And what happened?"

The girl is more relaxed than the first teenager. She tells Dr. Ruth that her best friend lied to her.

"Lied to you?" Dr. Ruth's voice rises and the "l" in "lied" has a lilting sound, almost a sing-song quality. "What did you do the first time that happened?" she asks.

The girl doesn't answer the question, but says lying isn't worth it because a lie is always found out by others. She continues, "My friend used to say she couldn't see me because she was busy. Actually, she was with someone else and . . . "

Dr. Ruth interrupts. "Let me guess. Was it a boy?"

The audience laughs, and in a soft voice the girl answers, "Yes."

With her blue eyes sparkling, Dr. Ruth says, "Everyone wants to hear that." Her giggle ripples through the room.

The audience laughs again, but not at the girl telling her story nor at Dr. Ruth. They understand the girl's pain.

Tossing her long dark hair back, the girl explains that the boy wasn't a very nice person, but she really liked her girlfriend. She even gave her girlfriend a key to her house. And then the girl brought her boyfriend to the house when nobody was home.

Audience disapproval rumbles through the studio.

In her European accent, Dr. Ruth exclaims "No! Not good! And what finally happened?"

"We had a big blowing-out."

"Did you hit her?" Dr. Ruth asks, looking intently at the girl.

"No. But she's not my friend anymore."

Dr. Ruth then asks if anyone in the audience has ever had a fistfight with a friend.

A girl tells about an argument she had with her best friend in the school hallway that ended in a real fistfight.

"What about the guys here?" Dr. Ruth asks.

A boy raises his hand. He says, "I had a best friend that"—his voice cracks—"that stole my girlfriend."

The audience laughs as if they know where he's coming from, and the young man grins.

Another boy, his hair in a ponytail, tells about his best friend who steals from him. Dr. Ruth asks him if he's talked with his parents about this. He says that his mother and he talked, and she didn't want him to hang around with that particular friend anymore.

One girl, wearing thick horn-rimmed glasses, tells about being extra nice to a new girl in school because she remembered how she felt when she was a new student in an unfamiliar school. She says, "The girl seemed to like me, but when she got acquainted with other kids, she just dropped me like . . . like I was nobody."

Dr. Ruth asks her what she did about that.

"We had a fight. You know, just a word fight. And I told her to just forget about being friends."

Another girl tells about her best friend who got a boyfriend. She says, "Then the best friend acted like I was a disease."

Dr. Ruth understands about friends and friendships because they have played a very important part in her life. She tells her young audience (and also writes in her and Dr. Nathan Kravetz' book *First Love: A Young People's Guide to Sexual Information*) that true friends do not take advantage of each other. She says a friend is someone who likes you even when for some reason you are not likeable. A friend backs you up, is your pal, your rooting section. Friends borrow from and lend to each other. A friend supports you when you have problems and celebrates your successes with you. And a friend is trustworthy.

What if the friendship seems one-sided, with one person giving to the relationship and the other taking from it? Or perhaps one person in the friendship decides to get into shoplifting, drugs, or casual sex. What then? Dr. Ruth says then it's time to back out of the gone-sour friendship.

More hands go up. Everybody seems eager to tell Dr. Ruth about experiences with best friends. And this is one of Dr. Ruth's gifts—drawing people out through her down-to-earth and reassuring manner in talking with them. She doesn't preach at them. She makes them feel better. She encourages them to respect themselves and others.

What is there about this energetic, constantly moving, tiny woman that puts young people at ease and allows them to share their disappointments and sometimes pain with friendships?

Perhaps it is her shortness in height that makes her seem more like them or perhaps it is the way she listens with her complete attention on them. Possibly it is her European accent that disarms them. More likely, it is because Dr. Ruth does not moralize or make judgmental comments to her young audience that they feel comfortable, more open, and less self-conscious.

Dr. Ruth has a way about her that makes the teenagers feel as if they are talking to their best friend. But probably the most important reason for Dr. Ruth's success with young people is her ability to listen with her heart.

Dr. Ruth not only talks with young people on her television show but also "talks" with them in the book, *First Love*. In this book she answers questions about the physical and mental changes that take place in maturing young adults. Despite the fact that our society is becoming more open and frank, there are still concerns that puzzle or worry teenagers, concerns that perhaps they don't feel comfortable discussing with their parents.

Some years ago, a favorite aunt or grandparent often lived with the family. The son or daughter in the family felt comfortable asking that special relative questions about growing up. Extended families for the most part do not exist in our society today. Often both parents work, and there never seems to be a right time to discuss the facts of life.

Or perhaps the dad has a fatherly talk with his son. Later, the son has another question, but either the father is on his way to work or involved in a home project or just plain tired and not interested in further discussion. So what does the boy do? He talks with his peers. Sometimes misinformation supplied by one's friends or even parents is passed along because of lack of knowledge.

In frank, easy-to-understand language, either written or spoken, Dr. Ruth gives basic information regarding anatomy and sexual behavior. She dispels myths and encourages those with questions to seek answers from their parents, the school nurse, physician, or a psychotherapist like herself.

Dr. Ruth also receives hundreds of letters a week from young people asking a myriad of questions. Dr. Ruth answers the letters and gives down-to-earth advice. If the writer has a serious personal problem that is impossible to answer by mail, Dr. Ruth suggests the person contact his doctor or counselor or whoever could deal best with the situation. But always, Dr. Ruth keeps the good of the letter-writer in mind.

One fifteen-year-old girl writes and asks if there is something wrong with her. She doesn't want a boy touching her everywhere. She likes to hold hands and be kissed, but that is all.

Dr. Ruth says that there is nothing wrong with just holding hands and kissing. She cautions everyone not to be pressured into doing anything more than he or she wants to do.

Another girl writes that her girlfriend is very "loving" with lots of boys. The letter-writer wonders if she would be more popular if she were, you know, loving.

According to Dr. Ruth, no one should have to merchandise her body in order to be popular. The girl who barters her physical love for a boy's company puts little value on herself. Often, her so-called popularity is short-lived. And often a girl who has been "loving" with lots of boys, ends up feeling unwanted and unworthy.

A young man writes that his friend thinks he might have V.D. (venereal disease) and does not know how to treat it. What should the friend do?

Dr. Ruth replies that the first thing the friend must do is hike himself off to the doctor for proper diagnosis and treatment. She explains that V.D. isn't like a sore throat or a sprained wrist. It doesn't heal itself. Further, she urges that the young man tell his parents of his illness.

The above questions are a few examples of those asked in the many letters that Dr. Ruth receives. Dr. Ruth believes that sex education is essential for making people's lives happier and safer.

Knowledge is a protection against unwanted pregnancies, sexually transmitted diseases, and acquired immune deficiency syndrome (AIDS). Dr. Ruth recognizes that peer pressure can be a mighty motivator. She urges young people to belong to and enjoy being part of a group but to think for themselves and not be pressured into doing something because friends are doing it.

Dr. Ruth does not promote indiscriminate, casual relationships. She believes strongly in marriage and family. In the book *First Love*, and her radio and television talks, she stresses the need for love, caring, and healthy relationships based on trust.

She understands about struggles, disappointments, heartaches. She also knows from experience that sometimes one is "laid flat" by some horrendous happening, and she knows the only thing to do is get up and get going again. She likens herself to the German doll *Stehaufmannchen*, which, when it is laid flat, stands right up again because of the weight in its base.

Dr. Ruth has traveled a long and difficult road to get where she is today. But, most importantly, she remembers where she was yesterday.

2

A Girl Named Karola Ruth Siegel

Dr. Ruth Westheimer was born in Frankfurt, Germany, on June 4, 1928. Her parents named her Karola Ruth Siegel. As a little girl, Karola wanted an older brother very much. While still very young, only six or seven years old, she believed that a stork could grant her wish. To encourage the stork's visit to her house, she put two lumps of sugar on the windowsill. But though the sugar lumps were gone in the morning, the big bird never left an older brother or even a baby. Karola was the only child her Orthodox Jewish parents would ever have.

One day Karola found a book hidden away in her parents' closet. The book was *Ideal Marriage*. From its pages Karola discovered that the stork had nothing to do with bringing babies. It was all up to a man and a woman. From that time on, Karola was interested in learning more about relationships.

Karola's early childhood was a happy one. She lived in a middle-class neighborhood. Her father, Julius Siegel, was a wholesaler in notions, such as buttons, needles, thread, and handkerchiefs. Each workday, he loaded his supplies onto his bicycle and peddled the notions to the various small stores in the surrounding area.

Julius Siegel, short and slight of build, was an only child, too. His father had died the year before Karola was born. His mother, Selma Siegel, shared a ground-floor apartment in the northern part of the city of Frankfurt with him, his wife, and Karola.

Grandma Selma was a set-in-her-ways, domineering woman. She wore her thin white hair in a tight bun on top of her head. As she walked, her long dark skirt flounced in a no-nonsense way about her feet. She resented her son's having to marry Karola's mother, Irma Hanauer, because Irma was pregnant. After all, Irma was just a farm girl who worked as a housekeeper for the Siegel family. Julius Siegel, in his mother's opinion, was really marrying below his class. The tension between Grandma Selma

Downtown Frankfurt, Germany as it appeared before World War II.

and her daughter-in-law Irma was as much a part of Karola's home environment as the love that each woman felt for the child.

And Karola was much loved, too, by her mother's parents, Moses and Pauline Hanauer. They lived some fifty miles outside of Frankfurt in a small village called Wiesenfeld. Karola's Grandpa Moses was a very religious man. He was a cattle dealer, but he managed his business affairs poorly. Often, he would sell a calf or cow and neglect to ask for payment. Grandma Pauline, the mother of six children, was a happy, pretty woman, and the men in the small community liked to tease and flirt with her. Both Grandpa Moses and Grandma Pauline were very short.

Probably because of Grandma Selma's resentment of her, Irma went to her parents' home for the birth of her child. Irma remained at her parents' farm until Karola was a year old. During that first year, her father journeyed there every weekend to see his wife and baby daughter.

Even after she and her mother returned to Frankfurt to live in the Siegel family quarters, they still vacationed at Grandpa Moses and Grandma Pauline's whenever possible. Karola liked visiting Wiesenfeld because it was a small community. And she particularly liked her mother's sisters and brothers and their children who lived in the area. Her grandparents' farm with its cows, chickens, and geese delighted Karola.

Still, she was happy in her city home in Frankfurt and her own neighborhood of four-story red brick row houses. The Siegel apartment consisted of four rooms. Karola's parents had one room for their bedroom with a small alcove off it for Karola's bed. Notions and supplies for her father's business took up another room. The third room was both a living room and Grandma Selma's bedroom, and the fourth room was the kitchen.

The backyard was grassy, with many flowers. Long clotheslines stretched the length of the yard. All the people in the building had specific days on which to use a common laundry room, so wet clothes were constantly hanging on the line. Because Karola was so tiny, her mother often put her in the laundry basket so that she would be safe while her mother hung the family wash. Since their apartment was rather dark, Karola liked laundry day in the sunny backyard.

There was a Catholic hospital nearby and a Jewish cemetery just north of her home. At the end of her block was a wonderful small park with many old chestnut trees. Karola often played on the slides and swings or built castles in the sandbox in the shady, quiet park. On the edge of the park was a small store that sold household necessities. But more importantly to Karola, the store sold candy in the shape of teddy bears and chocolate-covered pastry with whipped cream.

Sometimes Karola's father rode her around the park on his bicycle, which he had modified so that Karola could sit on a seat resting on the bar of the bike. Because Karola was so small for her age, she could not reach the pedals to ride by herself. As the two of them biked through the park, her father drilled her on the multiplication tables. Since Karola wasn't even in school yet, this was quite an accomplishment and one that later proved to be her salvation.

Most evenings the Siegel family spent in the living room. Karola's mother and grandma sewed and Karola and her father read. Sometimes, when her father leaned over to help her with a difficult word, his moustache tickled the nape of her neck. Later, from her bed in the alcove of her parent's bedroom, Karola watched as her father, propped up in his bed, read or said his prayers. Finally, she drifted off to sleep, content with her world.

Religion played a big part in Karola's life. The Siegel family were Orthodox Jews, which meant they followed the laws pertaining to diet and Sabbath. Every morning, Dr. Ruth writes in her autobiography *All in a Lifetime*, she watched her father put on phylacteries—the black cubes that Jewish men wear at morning services. The cubes contain Torah texts (laws from the Old Testament of the Bible).

On Friday evenings, Karola's father blessed her and then the two of them went to the synagogue. Ordinarily, only the boys and men attended the religious service while the women and girls stayed at home to prepare the evening meal. But Karola's father always took her for the service.

Karola loved going with her father to the beautiful synagogue. The men sat downstairs and the few women who attended sat in the gallery. The children were permitted to go back and forth between the men's place of worship and the women's.

Sometimes, Karola went with her father when he attended a small shul (synagogue) in the Jewish hospital near their home. They were always especially welcomed there because her father then helped fill the minyan, the minimum number of ten men that is necessary for prayer.

Hanukkah, the Feast of Dedication, was one of the special December Jewish holidays that Karola loved. Each night a candle was lit and presents given until the eighth night when all the candles were lit and glowing. This festival celebrated the victory over Syrian King Antiochus IV Epiphanes who had at one time tried to stamp out the Jewish faith. Karola loved the delicious cakes and sweets that were prepared for this joyful holiday.

Another celebration that Karola enjoyed was Purim. Purim occurs during the latter part of February or early March. It is a happy festival. There is a carnival feeling in the synagogue. Often the children have fancy dress parties or act out plays. Karola liked taking candy, fruit, and biscuits to friends and family. Purim commemorates the time when Esther and her cousin Mordecai saved the Jewish people from massacre. Haman, chief minister of the Persian King Xerxes, had cast lots to decide which day he would kill the Jews. But Esther, at great risk to herself, begged the king to spare the Jewish people. The king did, and Haman was hanged.

On this day, Karola's mother made little gingerbread men with raisins for buttons. The gingerbread men represented Haman, the villain, of the Purim story.

Rosh Hashanah, which is celebrated in the seventh month of the Hebrew lunar calendar and on the first day of the rise of the new moon, was a religious New Year celebration that Karola particularly liked. First, the people in the synagogue said prayers of repentance. Then the rabbi blew the shofar (ram's horn). The shofar trumpeted the call for spiritual awakening. Of all the cakes and sweets served during this celebration, honey cake was Karola's favorite. Ten days after Rosh Hashanah, Jews celebrated Yom Kippur. This is a day of atonement, for righting wrongs within the Jewish communities. The Siegel's faith was both a source of religious education and social contact for Karola.

Another joy in Karola's early life was school. Weeks before the term began, she played school until she practically wore out her satchel for carrying books, her box of chalk, and the small blackboard and sponge.

She was enrolled in Frankfurt's select Samson Raphael Hirsch School, an all-girls' school. Although there was another Jewish school that was less expensive and closer to Karola's home, Grandma Selma insisted that the Samson Raphael Hirsch School was *the* place for Karola to obtain the correct Orthodox Jewish training.

School was everything Karola had expected. She loved learning; she loved recess where they played hopscotch or jumped rope or traded doll pictures (like young people trade baseball cards today). And she loved making new friends. Friends were very important to her in school and, in fact, all through her life. Her interest in people was broad and inquisitive. Even as a young girl, Karola was curious as to why an individual was happy or sad and how she could help that person. Karola was a good friend to people, and in turn, she had loyal friends. One girl, Mathilde, was particularly special to Karola. She didn't know it then, but their friendship would provide comfort and love when all the world seemed full of hate.

But Karola almost was taken out of first grade. A few weeks after school had begun, a doctor came to the classroom to examine the children. When he saw tiny Karola, he turned to the teacher and said that this child didn't belong in first grade. Thinking quickly, Karola began reciting the multiplication tables she had learned while riding on the bike with her father. The doctor was impressed, and tiny Karola was allowed to remain in first grade in spite of her size. This ability to think quickly under stressful conditions has helped Karola throughout her life.

Until she was ten years old, Karola's only concern was her size. She was shorter than all of her friends and the shortest youngster in her class at school. Because fish oil was thought by many people to promote growth and general good health in young people, many parents gave their children a spoonful of fish oil each day. Karola's parents doubled the dose because they hoped it would make her grow taller. It didn't. Karola was destined always to be smaller than average.

But though Karola's world was sheltered and filled with love, the world around her was contaminated with hate. Just three years before Karola was born, thirty-six-year-old Adolph Hitler planted the seeds of evil in his book, *Mein Kampf.* This book, part autobiography, part political dogma, and in major part an outlet for his deep-rooted hatred of Jews, was written while he was serving time in jail for his participation in an attempted overthrow of the government. Upon his release from jail, Hitler reorganized the Nazi party. By 1933, he was the leader of the Nazi party, and President Paul von Hindenburg appointed him chancellor of Germany.

This appointment gave Hitler the power to carry out his evil plans against Jews. First, he removed Jews from civil service jobs. Then he stripped them of all their civil rights. Jewish teachers lost their jobs and Jewish students were prohibited from attending the universities. When Jewish students demonstrated against Hitler's edict, storm troopers (Hitler's private Nazi army) attacked them with batons. Jews were banned from other professions and, many times, Jewish businesses were taken over by German interests. Further, Hitler encouraged the German people to harass the Jewish population by shoving them from the sidewalk or spitting at them. He passed laws that forbade his "master race Aryans" from associating with or marrying Jews.

But Karola's knowledge of the growing Nazi nightmare was limited. Besides being young and unaware of world events, she seemed to be insulated from the escalating horror by her family, her religion, her school. Even her neighborhood, because of its mix of Gentiles and Jews, protected her from discrimination because the Gentiles were not only neighbors but friends who liked the Siegels for themselves.

But, soon, nothing—not family, religion, school, or neighborhood—could protect Karola from the mass persecution of the Jews that enveloped the country and changed Karola's life forever.

3

Kristallnacht

Each day the tempo of hatred of Jews in Germany increased. By 1938, even the young people like Karola were aware of the tension that had invaded their lives. For instance, Karola knew that her father's notions business had fallen off. She wasn't certain whether it was because of the poor economy in Germany as Grandma Selma and her parents explained or whether it was because of the growing oppression Jews were experiencing.

At the synagogue she overheard men talking about the situation. One man said, "So what else is new? Jews have always been persecuted. This reign of intolerance will pass." But others believed that the worst was yet to come. And they were right.

On September 30, 1938, British Prime Minister Neville Chamberlain along with French Premier Édouard Daladier met with Hitler in what became known as the Munich Conference. At this meeting an agreement was signed that allowed Hitler and Germany to annex the Sudetenland of Czechoslovakia on October 1. In return, Hitler promised not to claim any more Czechoslovakian territory. Since neither Britain nor France was prepared to fight a war with Germany, giving in to Hitler's demands seemed a small price to pay. But a far greater price was yet to be paid.

While Prime Minister Chamberlain and Premier Daladier were negotiating for "peace in our time," other people of various nations were trying to solve the Jewish refugee problem. They had read about Germany's depriving Jews of their civil rights and had heard about how Jews were being harassed and mistreated. President Franklin D. Roosevelt invited thirty-three governments to meet and, in a cooperative effort, aid in the emigration of Jewish refugees from Germany. On July 6, 1938, the refugee conference met at Évian-les-Bains, a luxurious resort on the French shore of Lake Geneva. At this meeting, called the Évian Conference, representatives of thirty-one nations and thirty-nine private charitable organizations expressed sympathy for the Jews persecuted by Hitler's regime. But no nation threw open its borders. No nation was willing to welcome more than a few thousand Jewish immigrants.

On October 28, 1938, one month after the Munich agreement was signed and several months after the Évian Conference, German troops launched an assault against the Polish Jews living in Germany. Without warning, the Nazis snatched the children of Polish Jews from city streets and threw them into trucks and trains bound for the Polish border. Jewish families of Polish ancestry, their aged, and their sick were also rounded up and placed with the abducted children on the trucks and trains. The Jews were allowed only the clothes on their back and ten marks, which, at that time, was equivalent to four American dollars.

Bewildered and frightened, the captives clung to each other as the trucks and trains sped through the bitter cold night—destination unknown. At the Polish border station of Zbaszyn, a no-man's-land between the German and Polish frontiers, the Nazi soldiers dumped their human cargo of over 18,000 Polish Jews. The desperate people sought shelter in empty railroad cars and abandoned, heatless barracks. Food was scarce. Shelter was inadequate. Clothing was ill-suited to the harsh conditions.

News of the plight of the Jewish deportees reached the world and particularly the Jews living in Germany. Rabbis in the various German synagogues urged people to donate clothing, food, and money for the victims. German Jews, because of their cultural background, had always felt superior to the Polish Jews. But the brutal treatment of the Polish Jews at the hands of the German troops erased all feelings of snobbery or class distinction from the German Jews' hearts. The deportees were human beings as well as fellow Jews. Many charitable drives were held to benefit the persecuted Polish Jews. Karola helped Grandma Selma and her mother gather some of their extra clothing to give to the unfortunate deportees.

The brutal deportation of the Polish Jews was the first of a string of events in a campaign against the Jews that shocked the world and changed the course of Karola's life.

It so happened that Zindel Grynszpan and his family, except for one son who had fled to France earlier, were among the Polish Jews banished to the border station of Zbaszyn. When seventeen-year-old Herschel Grynszpan received a letter from his father describing the family's suffering, he was overwhelmed with grief and anger and he bought a pistol.

On November 7, 1938, Herschel Grynszpan went to the German embassy in Paris. At the embassy, Grynszpan demanded to see Ambassador Johannes von Velczeck. But instead of the German ambassador meeting with Grynszpan, Ernst vom Rath, a minor official, was delegated to speak with the visitor.

As vom Rath walked toward the young man, Grynszpan, believing he was the ambassador, drew his pistol and shot vom Rath several times. Ironically, vom Rath was one of the few German officials in the Nazi party who was sympathetic to the Jews.

Grynszpan was taken into custody by the French police. At the police station Grynszpan collapsed and cried. "Being a Jew is not a crime," he said. "I am not a dog. I have a right to live, and the Jewish people have a right to exist on this earth. . . . "

On the afternoon of November 9th, Ernst vom Rath died of his gunshot wounds.

At two o'clock the next morning, the Nazi regime began a supposedly spontaneous orgy of arson, looting, murder, and arrests. With demonic enthusiasm, they burned 195 synagogues and looted over 7,500 Jewish businesses and shops. They completely destroyed more than 800 businesses and shops. Glass from the shattered shop windows littered the streets. The disaster became known as Kristallnacht, the "night of the broken glass."

Kristallnacht, the "night of the broken glass."

The Nazis in some communities arrested every male Jew. In all, some 20,000 Jews—men, women, and children—ended up in concentration camps as a result of Kristallnacht. German officials reported that thirty-five Jews were killed during the disaster, although news reporters and diplomatic observers stated that the number of deaths was much higher. In addition to the destruction of businesses and the murder of many Jews, the Germans levied a fine of one billion marks against all German Jews as restitution for the murder of Ernst vom Rath by the Polish Jew Herschel Grynszpan.

The Nazis then enforced even stricter restrictions on the Jews. No longer were they allowed on certain streets. They were barred from public parks and many public buildings.

Still, Hitler was not satisfied. He wanted to rid Europe of its 9.6 million Jewish inhabitants. Thousands were sent to concentration camps where they worked as slave laborers for Germany. Other Jews were rounded up and herded into trucks supposedly to be resettled in another area; instead they were driven into the country where they were made to take off their clothes and then were marched into pits and shot. The pits were then filled with lime and covered over. Before Hitler's reign of terror was over, more than six million Jews would lose their lives in the ghettos of Eastern Europe, in slave labor camps, "resettlement programs," or the gas chambers at concentration camps.

Although ten-year-old Karola did not know of the atrocities being committed against the Jews, she knew that bad things were going on because her beautiful synagogue had been burned down. And her school was closed. But she wasn't sure why. Several months earlier, classes had stopped because of a polio outbreak. Perhaps there was another epidemic, and when it was over, school would begin again. Although she didn't understand the full meaning of what was happening, she saw the anxious expressions on her family's faces, heard their strained conversations and felt the tension in her home.

Kristallnacht included the burning of many Jewish businesses.

While taking a walk on November 15, six days after Kristall-nacht, Karola and her father stopped and visited with different acquaintances. Everyone they talked with mentioned the terrifying "night of the broken glass." One man said that Karola's family should get out of Germany. The man warned, "Kristallnacht is just the beginning. More terrible things are going to happen to the Jews."

According to Dr. Ruth's autobiography, Karola's father didn't believe anything terrible would happen. At least, not the next day because it was a Catholic holiday.

The next morning, however, there was a knocking at the Siegels' door. Several big men in brown-shirted uniforms and

After Kristallnacht, Nazi's designated which shops were Jewish by writing "Jude" on the windows.

shiny black boots entered. They wore swastikas on their left sleeves and carried guns, which were tucked inside their wide black belts. Karola was frightened. Although the soldiers didn't hit or abuse anyone, they demanded that her father come with them.

Karola's mother began to cry. This frightened Karola even more, and she burst into tears.

The soldiers ordered Karola to stop her bawling. Then they turned to her father and told him, "You will come with us."

"Wait," Grandma Selma said. She reached inside the seam of her long dark skirt and took out some money. She handed it to one of the uniformed men and begged them to take care of her son.

Karola watched her father, slightly bent, but head held high, walk out of the apartment to a big noisy truck idling at the curb. There were other men in the truck. Before climbing into the back of the truck, her father turned and waved. He looked as if he were trying to smile. All Karola saw was the anguish on his face.

The soldiers got into the truck cab and sped away. Shocked, Karola watched until the truck was out of sight. Why would soldiers take her dear father away as if he were a criminal? Was this terrifying scene a dream? Would she wake up and discover that this was just a nightmare?

In the apartment, no one said a word. Silence hung in the room like a shroud of death. Each of them—Grandma Selma, Karola's mother, and Karola herself—went off by themselves. Although they were Jews, they were German. And, as was mentioned in Dr. Westheimer's book, *All in a Lifetime,* it wasn't the German way to show emotion.

At the same time the Nazis were persecuting the Jews in Germany, their armies were invading Austria, Czechoslovakia, Poland, the Netherlands, and France. In June 1941, they launched a full-scale invasion of Russia. Wherever the Nazi troops went, they carried Hitler's hatred of the Jews with them. Jews all over Europe suffered from the Nazis' persecution.

Later, Karola learned that her father had been taken to a detention camp. At this time, detention camps were merely locations where Jews were taken as punishment for being Jews. After a period of time, many of the Jews were allowed to return to their homes. Later, these camps became the infamous concentration camps.

Hitler's regime imprisoned as many Jews as the camps would hold. Many of the prisoners died from the hardships they suffered in the camps. And the Nazis tried to drive the Jews who weren't detained in camps out of the country by depriving them of their means of earning a living and by making their lives as unpleasant as possible.

At Karola's home, days, then weeks passed in silent sorrow. Karola tried not to talk about her father because she knew it upset her mother and Grandma Selma. So each of them carried her burden of grief without tears or complaints. Karola's mother and Grandma Selma seemed to have called a truce in their previous stormy relationship. Karola noticed that the petty arguments and disagreements between them had disappeared and were replaced with shared concern over husband/son.

When Hanukkah came, Karola took over her father's responsibility. She lit the candles on each of the eight nights. But the holiday wasn't the same without her gentle father.

Each night she prayed that God would watch over her father and send him home.

4

Kinder Transport

Karola dreaded the nights. Although her mother continued the habit of lying with her daughter until she fell asleep, it wasn't the same to Karola. She missed seeing her father propped up in his bed, reading or praying. Many times during the nights that followed her father's forced departure, needing closeness and comfort, she left her bed in the alcove and climbed in with her mother. The continuing love of her family helped shield her against the growing hatred of the outside world.

After Kristallnacht, classes did not begin again at school. The synagogue had been destroyed, and worship took place in makeshift surroundings. And with her father gone, Karola felt a bleak emptiness in her life that defied comfort. She tried not to talk about her father because just the mention of his name caused pain to her mother and Grandma Selma. But still, memories of him lit up her thoughts and lessened the sorrowful shadows around her heart.

One night, about five weeks after her father had been taken away to the detention camp, her mother and Grandma Selma came into Karola's alcove. Her mother sat on one side of her bed and Grandma Selma on the other.

Each woman reached for one of her hands. Then, in a solemn voice, her mother told her that she was to be part of the Kinder Transport. This meant that she would join a group of German Jewish children who were to be taken to Switzerland.

Karola began to cry. She didn't want to leave her mother or Grandma Selma. Once before, she had gone to a summer camp, and she had been so very homesick. Why would they send her away again? And what about her father?

Grandma Selma explained that only about one hundred children from Frankfurt would be allowed to go on this journey. She said that the delegates of the thirty-one nations who had met in Évian, France in July, 1938, came up with this plan to help the Jews. By having a certain number of their children taken into France, England, Belgium, or Switzerland, the parents of these children would have time to get the necessary papers to escape Germany and emigrate to another country.

Her mother said that she would only be in Switzerland for about six months. By then, perhaps the bad things happening to Jews would be over. Irma Siegel assured her daughter that they would come and get her soon.

Karola covered her ears with her hands. She didn't want to hear anymore. She didn't want to leave her mother or Grandma Selma. She didn't want to abandon her loving home for an unfamiliar destination.

Gently, Grandma Selma pulled her hands from her ears. She said that Switzerland was a good place to visit because it had the finest chocolate in the world.

Karola shook her head.

Her mother told her that Mathilde, her best friend, was lucky, too. She also had been chosen to join the Kinder Transport children. "You and the other children will be well taken care of," she said.

Still, Karola did not want to go.

A few days later, a letter came from her father. He was in the Buchenwald detention camp. In the letter, he wrote that he would feel much better if Karola would agree to go to Switzerland.

With tears streaming down her cheeks, she said she would go. As an adult and a mother, Dr. Westheimer now appreciates the supreme sacrifice her parents made. She knows they sent her away because they loved her so much. Until she had her own children, she didn't understand such unselfish love.

But before a child could be part of the Kinder Transport, there were several requirements to be met. First, she or he had to be under sixteen years of age. Second, the individual had to be of German Jewish ancestry. Third, the person must either be an orphan or have a father in a detention camp. Finally, a physician licensed to care for the medical needs of Jews exclusively must give a written statement that the individual was not ill either physically or mentally. Karola met all these requirements.

A month after her physical examination, word came that the Kinder Transport children were to report the next day to a Frankfurt orphanage located near the city's railroad station. Karola would spend the night with the other children at the orphanage. She was advised to bring only one suitcase.

That night Grandma Selma sat on the side of Karola's bed. Not looking at her, Grandma Selma said there were certain things she wanted to tell Karola about growing up.

Karola said that there was no need to explain anything. After all, she had read parts of the marriage manual and had talked with her friends at school. She already knew about such things. Obviously relieved, Grandma Selma stood up and with a quick kiss on Karola's forehead, left the alcove.

The next morning Karola tearfully packed her clothes, some chocolate candies, and a doll into her bag. She also was allowed to bring one article from the house. She tossed in a wash cloth. Years later, she wondered why she had chosen such an item. She could

Karola's father was taken to the Buchenwald detention camp in 1938. It later became the Buchenwald concentration camp, pictured here.

have brought the Sabbath candlesticks or a special dish or pictures of the family. But at that time she was ten years old. She didn't know that six months away from her family would stretch into forever.

Her mother and Grandma Selma took Karola by streetcar to the Frankfurt orphanage, where she spent the night with the other children bound for Switzerland.

The night at the orphanage seemed endless to Karola. The children were crowded together on cots and sleeping mats. It was so different from her own bed in the alcove at home. And the smell of fear hung like smoke in the roomful of huddled children.

Some of the children were a few years younger than Karola and others were a few years older. But when the lights were turned off for the night, they were all children leaving home and loved ones. In the darkness, the sound of quiet sobs mingled with the creaking of the old building.

At the first light of day, people in charge of the Kinder Transport herded the children to the railroad station a few blocks away. The sky was overcast and misty. The only sound in the early morning was the shuffling of feet on the sidewalk as the children walked along the familiar streets of Frankfurt toward an uncertain future.

At the train station, mothers and other relatives and friends waited to say goodbye. There were no fathers there. A huge train engine with ghostly steam hovering above it hissed on the tracks.

Mother and Grandma Selma waited at the railroad station for one last goodbye. Then it was time to board the train. Mother told her to be a good girl. She assured the frightened child that they would see each other again soon.

Grandma Selma folded her in her arms and whispered to her to trust in the almighty God.

Karola boarded the train and took the window seat next to Mathilde. Eagerly she pressed her face against the windowpane hoping to see her family waiting on the station platform. When she saw them, she rapped on the window and waved. She tried to smile as her father had when he was taken away. The sound of the train whistle startled her. Then, with a jerk, the wheels of the locomotive began to turn.

She watched through her window as her mother and Grandma Selma tried to keep up with the train as it made its way out of the station. The train moved slowly at first, then gradually gained speed. The last, tear-blurred view of her family was of her mother running alongside the track, with Grandma Selma, her long skirts flapping about her legs, right behind her. It was the first time and the last time Karola ever saw her Grandma Selma run.

As she lost sight of her family, held-back tears rolled down her cheeks. She looked about the train, all strangers except for Mathilde. From her bag Karola took out her doll and held it close. The doll, like Mathilde, helped comfort her.

The train steamed toward the Swiss border town of Basel. As the train moved through mountain passes and across fast-flowing rivers, Karola's friendliness and natural cheerfulness bubbled up. She talked to those around her and then she got everyone singing familiar Hebrew songs.

About noontime, they reached the town of Basel. The older children, about fifty of them, got off the train to be housed and cared for there. The rest of the children were given a hot drink and a snack. Then they were off again, heading toward the village of Rorschach. There they changed trains for the final leg of their journey.

It was late afternoon when the train pulled into the mountain village of Heiden, their destination. One by one the children, their lone piece of luggage in hand, disembarked from the train. The people in charge of the Kinder Transport led the fifty young people through the town.

Karola enjoyed walking through the quaint village. The ginger-bread chalets with their wide eaves and sloping roofs were so different from the Frankfurt row houses. Snow dusted the many evergreen bushes and trees scattered along the way. Looking beyond the small town, she saw a large body of water. Later, she learned that this was Lake Constance, and it bordered Germany, Switzerland, and Austria.

Several times as she walked along the streets of Heiden, she caught glimpses of people peeking out windows, curious to see this group of "imported" children. But nobody rushed out to greet them. When the church bells began to ring, Karola first thought it was to welcome them, but she was wrong. The bells chimed the hour.

They walked down a slight slope for about a half a mile until they came to two buildings. One building was quite large and ornate while the other was much smaller and looked more like a farm building. She later learned that the annex, as the smaller building was called, had once been a barn.

They entered the smaller building where a woman directed the young people to leave their bags and come with her. Karola didn't want to leave her one bag. That was all she had of home. But she did as she was told. The woman led them up some stairs to the second story. The upstairs was divided into six rooms—a room each for the older boys, younger boys, older girls, and younger girls. The other two rooms were for the adults who worked at the home.

Karola looked around the room with its row of cots. There was nothing about the room that was homelike. In a no-nonsense voice the woman explained that this was where they would sleep, that the toilets and showers were downstairs as well as the hall where they would eat and play.

After the woman went downstairs, Karola ran to the window and looked out. Snow with tufts of shrubbery peeking through quilted the surrounding acres. Karola saw a slide and swings. Several picnic tables and benches were scattered about the grounds. A quaint gazebo nestled among the trees. Such a beautiful area. So quiet and peaceful. It was hard to remember that bad things were happening in Germany.

In the distance, she heard a cow bell. Looking across the way, she saw a farm with cows in its pastures. Memories of her grand-parents' farm in Wiesenfeld tiptoed into her thoughts, awakening her feeling of loneliness.

After a light supper downstairs, the young people were told to wash and go to bed. Upstairs in the dorm room, the girls discovered a hole in the floor. Apparently this opening was to allow heat from the wood-burning stove in the room below to rise to the second-story room. Naturally, the girls peeked through the hole.

As Karola peered through the opening, she saw the people in charge of the home rummaging through the young people's bags. Every so often, they'd pull out a dress or blouse from someone's luggage and laugh because it was worn or unfashionable.

When her luggage was opened, Karola held her breath and watched as one of the women pawed through her things. When she came across the chocolate that Karola's mother and Grandma Selma had given her, the woman smacked her lips. Then she passed the candy to the other adults.

Karola didn't understand why these people would eat her chocolate. After all, Grandma Selma had said that there was lots of chocolate in Switzerland. But she said nothing.

One thing became painfully clear. Her stay here was going to be more difficult than any summer camp ever could be. By nature Karola was a cheerful, happy child who adapted to new situations well. She knew she had no choice but to accept whatever the Swiss orphanage decided, so she might as well make the best of it. After all, Switzerland was a beautiful country. She was safe, and soon her family would be coming for her.

But that night, in spite of the beauty of the place and her natural joy in living and the sense of safety the orphanage provided, she cried herself to sleep.

5

Wartheim

The name of the Swiss orphanage was Wartheim, which is German
for "waiting home." And wait the German Jewish young people did.
Waited for news of the war. Waited for letters from relatives.
Waited to emigrate. Karola waited at the orphanage for more than
six long years.

To these young people the meaning of Wartheim, "waiting
home" meant more than an interval of time. It also meant waiting
on or serving the Swiss children who were at the home because they
were orphans or had divorced parents or were at the home for a
holiday. From the very beginning of their stay at Wartheim, the
Kinder Transport group realized that they were not welcome guests
of Switzerland but foisted burdens. And although the Swiss Aid
Committee for Refugee Children was responsible for the children's
expenses, the personnel at the home reminded them of their obli-
gation to repay the Swiss government by working. The director of
the orphanage was quoted in *All in a Lifetime* as saying, "We took
you in. You're lucky to be alive."

A few days after they arrived at the orphanage, they were taken
to the Heiden town hall to obtain permits for their six-month stay

in Switzerland. Each Kinder Transport child was assigned a number and given a file in which his personal information was recorded. Karola's number was 855,555. In her file it stated that with the exception of her identity card, she had no other credentials. Further, she was in Switzerland only until emigration could be arranged by her Jewish parents.

Later, Karola discovered that the permits were to be renewed every six months. Permits were routinely renewed, but still the possibility of refusal crouched in the dark corners of the children's minds. To be sent back to Germany where horrible atrocities were being committed was a terrifying possibility. Consequently, the German Jewish children knew better than to grumble, to misbehave, or to cause any sort of disturbance.

Because they were set apart from the Swiss youngsters at the home and in the village of Heiden, the refugees provided support for each other. They continued to live in the Orthodox Jewish tradition in which they had been reared. They kept kosher by following the dietary laws of Judaism. They observed the Jewish holidays and said their Hebrew prayers.

The Swiss were well known for their extreme cleanliness. Very quickly Karola's life at the home became a routine of cleaning and scrubbing. Her day began at 6:30 A.M. when she rose from bed and dressed. At 7:00 A.M. she and the other girls her age woke the younger ones and helped them dress. At 7:30 Karola had her coffee, then she set the table for breakfast. After the meal she helped clear the table and tidy up. When her chores were finished, she attended school for a couple of hours. After lunch she put the younger children to bed for their naps. Then she attended school again until five in the afternoon. There were more chores of scrubbing and waxing after which it was time to help bathe the youngsters or do some mending. When dinner was over, she put the younger ones to bed. By 7:30 P.M. Karola herself was ready for bed.

On Fridays or during vacation time her routine varied slightly. Extra cleaning was done in the kitchen. After lunch, if the weather was nice, Karola was allowed to go swimming. By 3:00 P.M. she was at the home again and did some mending. In the evening, as usual, she helped bathe the children and after dinner she polished their shoes so that they would be spotless for Sabbath the next day.

Fortunately, Karola liked caring for the younger children. In fact, when she first arrived at the home, she was put in charge of a six-year-old boy. Later, Karola was the leader of a group of Boy Scouts. She took this responsibility seriously and drilled the boys on the Scout laws and oath so they would be letter-perfect. She also planned fun things for them to do, like hiking and swimming.

Often, Karola was in charge of younger girls. When one of them cried because she was homesick, Karola, to console her, gave the child the one doll she had brought from her Frankfurt home.

Karola sometimes paid extra attention to a younger child because the child's older brother asked her to. Although she truly loved little children, she also liked the boys of her own age. The Orthodox Jewish tradition was to have separate schools for boys and girls. But because two separate facilities would be too costly, this tradition was ignored at Wartheim. And Karola was glad. She liked to talk with the boys. She liked to be with them. And she liked to tease them.

One wintry night, she climbed out on the roof and rapped against the boys' dorm window to scare them. In attempting to open the window, the boys broke it. Someone tattled to Fraulein Risenfeld, a woman who helped care for the refugees, and she paddled Karola. Karola was indignant. She decided that Fraulein Risenfeld did not have a sense of humor.

To the refugee children, Fraulein Risenfeld was a miserable creature. She told the Jewish children that their parents couldn't have loved them very much because they had sent them away. She said that their parents were like some animals that eat their young.

She censored all letters the young people wrote and all letters they received.

One girl managed to mail a letter off to her parents without Fraulein Risenfeld's knowledge. The girl protested in the letter about some of the harsh treatment at the home. Fraulein Risenfeld read her parents' response and realized that the girl had complained. To punish her, Fraulein Risenfeld beat her in front of all the refugees. She ordered the children to shun this ungrateful girl and not to look at her or talk to her. Karola wondered why Fraulein Risenfeld was so mean. Was it because she didn't have a husband or even a boyfriend?

But in spite of the censorship, letters were the most important part of the children's lives. They were a link to their loved ones, their homeland, their past.

Karola's father, now released from the detention camp, often wrote his letters in verse. He did this because he could tell Karola more without being censored than if he wrote in prose. His letters were loving, cheerful, and full of praise for Karola's good grades.

The love that Grandma Selma felt for Karola was apparent in her letters. She wrote about religious holidays and how happy she was that her granddaughter was keeping the Jewish traditions in her life. Any hardships the family might be enduring under the Hitler regime were never mentioned. Often Grandma Selma included a bit of philosophy in her letters. Once she wrote that Frankfurt had had some snow. She exclaimed how beautiful it was, falling from the sky, and then added that it was only when the snow came in contact with people that it became ugly and dirty. Her letters always ended with admonitions for Karola to be healthy and cheerful and to be a good, thoughtful girl.

Letters from Karola's mother reflected her interest in her daughter's activities—the ski trips, her report cards, her friends. She complimented Karola on being a big girl because she sent New Year's greetings without being reminded.

In most of her letters to her family, Karola asked about emigration. When? And how much longer would she have to wait in the home? Karola had been there for two years when her mother wrote that there was no news on the family's emigration. She asked her daughter to be patient.

At the same time Grandma Selma wondered why she kept asking about emigration. She pointed out in her letters to Karola that she was well cared for and that the sky and sun were over all people everywhere. She advised her granddaughter to enjoy her youth and prepare herself for the arduous life in the future.

In her autobiography Dr. Westheimer noted two things about her letters from home. First, they all were stamped with a swastika seal. Second, the return name on the envelope from Grandma Selma now read Selma *Sara* Siegel. As an adult, she found out that the Nazis had ordered all Jewish women to use Sara as their middle name as a means of identifying them as Jews.

In rereading the letters in later years, Dr. Westheimer was startled to see how cheerful her loved ones were. In the midst of terror they wrote about everyday occurrences, about family, and friends, the weather. No mention was ever made of their persecution, of any hardships they were facing, or of concerns for their future welfare.

Why didn't they emigrate? First, Jews weren't allowed to leave the country without the proper papers. Second, Germany was Grandma Selma's home and she didn't want to leave until there was no choice. In one of her letters to Karola, she wrote that emigration was for young people. Even if her parents obtained proper papers, Karola's father was an only child. If his mother, Grandma Selma, refused to emigrate, he could not leave Germany and abandon her.

The last letter Karola received from her parents or Grandma Selma was written in September 1941. Later, she heard from friends in Frankfurt that the Siegels had emigrated, but they did not know where. Karola knew that when the war was over her parents would send for her. The news from her Frankfurt friends lifted her spirits, and she prayed that wherever her family was, they were well. Someone said that perhaps her family was in Poland. Karola wrote to Lodz, which was a Jewish ghetto in Poland, but she never received a reply. Her spirits sagged. She was finding it more and more difficult to keep believing her family was all right. A year later, Karola was relieved to receive a letter from her grandparents in Wiesenfeld in which they said her parents and grandma were safe. Again, like a yo-yo, her spirits were up. But after their letter, there was no further correspondence from any relatives or any news of her parents or grandparents. It was as if they all had disappeared into a bottomless hole. Karola felt as if a piece of her heart was missing.

In spite of the dark side of Karola's life, there was also a bright side—Max. She helped Max with his homework and knitted special apparel for him. And they talked. But her first love ended when she discovered Max kissing another girl.

Karola recovered from her blighted relationship quickly because now Putz came into her life. He was a year younger than Karola and had come to the home after having lived with several Swiss foster families first. He was handsome and intelligent and easy to talk to. Just being with him banished some of the foreboding thoughts she had about her family's welfare. Putz made her feel alive and worthy of admiration.

Together they figured out all kinds of ways of being alone. Sometimes Karola and her friend Marga would say they were going for a walk. Putz and Marga's boyfriend, Klaus, would also go for a walk. Then they would meet in the woods and pair up. At the home Putz and Karola hugged and kissed secretly under the staircase or behind an upstairs bedroom chimney.

About this time rumors spread throughout the home that Hitler was planning to invade Switzerland. This was a frightening prospect. From an upstairs window, Karola could see Germany just across Lake Constance. Invasion seemed a possibility. Although the refugees did not receive daily reports on the war, they were aware that Hitler had invaded Poland, Norway, and Denmark, and more recently the Netherlands, Belgium, and Luxembourg. Would Switzerland be next?

The people at the home advised their young charges that if such a terrible thing should happen, they were to go in groups of two into the mountains. Each couple consisted of an older child who would be responsible for her partner, a younger child.

But Karola and Putz had other ideas about escaping if the Germans invaded Switzerland. Together with their friends Klaus and Marga, they decided that the four of them would head for Spain and then on to Palestine.

Putz and Karola often talked about what they would do after the war. They drew house plans and talked about how they would furnish their own home. Always there was a children's room. Communal living had accentuated the need in their future lives to be a family.

Putz and Karola were a steady couple for almost three years. As Putz matured, he began to play up to one of the older women who worked at the home. Karola was jealous. Putz assured her he would always like her best. The final break came over a silly argument on how Putz should style his hair. He wanted to part it and comb it to the side. Karola wanted him to comb it straight back. They argued and Karola decided that the romance was over.

By this time Karola had been in Switzerland for three years. She was almost fourteen. Although when she was eight years old, she had secretly read passages from her parents' book, *Ideal Marriage,* and she had talked with different girls about life, there were many things about growing up that she didn't know.

Amazingly, it was Frau Risenfeld Neufeld who answered Karola's many questions. Frau Risenfeld Neufeld was now married and no longer the miserable creature she had been when the refugees first arrived. Karola was certain that having a mate was the reason for the radical change in her. Now she was understanding and easy to talk to. She answered Karola's questions about her maturing body in a straightforward manner. She explained how a child develops within the mother. She also suggested that Karola wear a bra.

A few weeks later, an inkling of Karola's future profession presented itself. She heard that someone had given one of the younger girls the wrong information about menstruation. Karola sat the young girl down and gave her the facts. In her autobiography there is an entry in Karola's diary in which she notes how bad it was to receive false information about these things.

Karola searched out books on sex education. When she didn't understand something she had read, she asked questions. Frau Berendt, a worker at the home, was especially helpful. The way she explained the facts of life made Karola realize that everything in nature was well-planned and ingenious. She remembered what Grandma Selma had said about snow being clean until it was made dirty by people. So it is with a relationship between a man and a woman. Sex is a natural act until some people make it dirty.

6

Graduation

By 1942, war raged across Europe. France had collapsed and England was under brutal and punishing attacks from Hitler's air force, the Luftwaffe. Hitler's armies had invaded Russia and advanced to the outskirts of Leningrad. Because of the attack on Pearl Harbor, the United States had declared war on Japan and joined England in its war against Germany and Italy. But the war in the Pacific was going badly for the Americans. French Indochina, the British colonies of Hong Kong and Singapore, the Dutch East Indies, and the Philippines all fell to Japanese forces. Japan then seized the Pacific Islands off the coast of Alaska. By early fall of 1942, the Japanese occupied a million square miles of territory in the Pacific.

More than three years had passed since Karola and the other Kinder Transport children had arrived at Wartheim. The older children were leaving the home to be on their own. This meant that now there was room for Karola and the other younger people in the main building. Set on several acres and surrounded by a lawn and beds of flowers, the old house was spectacular in the spring and summer months. Even in the cold season when the grounds were cloaked in winter's snowy wrap, the house was still impressive.

Built of wood with fantastic gables and intricate iron work, it stood three stories high. On the first floor there was a big kitchen plus showers, bathrooms, and bedrooms for the children. Each bedroom accommodated two or three people. There were more bedrooms on the second story as well as two small living rooms. Books and toys filled one living room while the other was furnished more as a parlor. The third floor had private rooms for the adults working at the home. The move from the annex to the house was a major improvement in the children's living quarters.

In 1942, fourteen-year-old Karola experienced another major change. For the first time since coming to Heiden, she was leaving it for ten whole days. Because she was still so short, the staff at the home decided that a doctor in Zurich might be able to give her hormone treatments to stimulate her growth.

Karola did not receive hormone injections, a fact for which she is thankful today. (Sometimes hormone treatments have side effects such as diabetes or excessive bone growth that causes deformities in the face, hands, and feet.) But she relished her ten days in Zurich. It reminded her of Frankfurt with its bustle of people and traffic and the many shops.

While in Zurich, she stayed at the home of Susie Guggenheim, a former Wartheim employee. On her first evening in the city, Susie brought her a little candy doll made out of marzipan, an almond paste, and served this delicacy to her in bed. Since there was no curfew for lights out as at the home, Karola read far into the night. All week long Karola, Susie, and Susie's boyfriend enjoyed the theater and concerts. On Friday evening, Susie told Karola to put her shoes outside her bedroom door and one of the servants would shine them. What a treat! She couldn't help but remember how many shoes she had shined at the home. On Sabbath morning she attended synagogue for the first time in four years.

Although her trip to Zurich was the high point of her stay at the home, there were other excursions and events in and around Heiden that she enjoyed. At the home she learned to appreciate what nature had to offer. The young people hiked through green meadows populated with wildflowers and up steep mountains that peaked in the clear, blue sky. The air had a vitality, a zest as they skied down the slopes or skated on frozen ponds. Ever since, the outdoors have proven to be a source of enjoyment for her.

And there was school. Karola hungered for knowledge. A room was set aside at Wartheim for classes. One teacher, Ignatz Mandel, taught forty youngsters ranging in age from six to fourteen. The children varied not only in their intelligence but also in the amount of their previous education. Ignatz Mandel, however, did the best he could by dividing the class into appropriate groups and then going from one group to the next to teach.

He obviously liked Karola. In her autobiography, *All in a Lifetime*, she gives his evaluation of her. He wrote: "Her general conduct is good. She is vivacious, has a good character. Very diligent. She has a good mind, which is sometimes impaired by too much impulsiveness. Very short, below average in height, but physical development is completely normal."

Another time, according to the *Current Biography Yearbook 1987*, the teacher noted on one of Karola's report cards that she was "very intelligent, very lively, and doesn't let anybody else talk."

Karola liked and admired Ignatz Mandel because of his dedication to his profession and his kindness to his students. She liked learning.

And she liked the visitors who came to the classroom. She looked forward to a particular Red Cross official's visit to check on conditions in the home because she thought he was fabulous (a favorite word of Karola's at this time), and he was so handsome.

Several representatives from a Zionist organization also came to talk to the students. The Zionist organization is a worldwide

Jewish movement first started with the goal of establishing a national homeland for the Jews in Palestine.

The people who ran Wartheim were not Zionists themselves. But they realized that when the war was over, most of their charges would probably emigrate to Palestine.

There was a reason for their belief. According to the agreement at the 1938 Évian Conference at which the Kinder Transport was arranged, refugees were not to be allowed to remain in their host countries. Consequently, refugees were to leave Switzerland after the war. Other Western European nations required that they have a relative already residing within their boundaries. There was a long waiting list for those wishing to emigrate to the United States. Consequently, the people of Wartheim encouraged the Zionist representatives to visit with the young people and tell them about Palestine.

The Zionist representatives were skilled in the art of persuasion. Many of them were extremely good-looking young men, which, for Karola, was an added incentive for emigrating to Palestine. They were adept at appealing to the young people's needs—their need to be wanted, to be useful, to have security, and a country of their own.

The representatives pointed out that living in kibbutzim (communities in which all production and economic activity is controlled by the state) was hard work. They pointed out that members of kibbutzim receive no salaries, only the necessities of life—food, clothing, medical care, and shelter. Once a year, members were given funds for a two-week vacation. But the representatives also gave the refugees Palestinian flags and showed them pictures of life in Palestine—pictures of smiling children, of people dancing, and of groves of olive trees. They told stories about the outstanding people who lived in kibbutzim. The representatives aroused in the adolescents a sense of responsibility to create a homeland for Jews.

To Karola the idea of going to Palestine was both challenging and rewarding. It filled a void in her, gave purpose to her life. Palestine would be her country, its people her people, its future her future. Besides, Uncle Lothar was in Palestine. She felt sure that if her parents were safe and eventually could emigrate, Palestine would be their choice for settlement.

For now, Karola needed to learn Hebrew in preparation for emigrating to Palestine. After the war and before becoming a part of a kibbutz, she and the other refugees would live in Erez, Palestine for six months. There they would learn everything they could about their new country before becoming a part of a community. The Zionist's cause inspired Karola and typically she embraced its philosophy wholeheartedly.

There were other visitors, too. Some French children, near starvation, came to the home for a short time. They had escaped from a Nazi labor camp in France where they had been miserably treated.

Later, some people from the Bergen-Belsen concentration camp (a camp located in Lower Saxony, a part of Germany) were at the home on a temporary basis. They told horror stories about the Nazis—about how they were conducting cruel medical experiments on their captives, how they were inflicting savage torture even on children, and how they were murdering thousands of people in gas chambers.

Surprisingly, the children at Wartheim had heard very little about the war or the atrocities going on around them. There was no radio at the home, and newspapers weren't available to the children. For some reason, the people at the home were reluctant to share much news about the war with the refugees. So the horror stories that the French children and the survivors of Bergen-Belsen concentration camp told stunned Karola. She knew that war was bloody and people got killed. But persecution, torture, and mass murder?

The suffering of the thousands of people made her feel insignificant. She also questioned whether she really wanted to be a Jew.

In the spring of 1943, her education at the home ended. Classes at the home only went to the eighth grade. Almost more than anything, Karola wanted to continue her education at the Heiden, Switzerland high school.

There were several reasons why this was not possible. First, the Orthodox Jewish tradition emphasized education for boys, but higher education for girls was a luxury. Second, it cost money to attend the high school in Heiden. Third, in the opinion of the director of the home, Karola was a "charity case" and was suited only to be trained as a maid.

April 8, 1943, was Karola's last day in school at the home. Although for some time she had fantasized about becoming a medical doctor, she realized that was an impossible dream. What to do? She knew she had to plan her own future.

It had been over two years since she had heard from her parents. She tried to keep believing they were safe—just unable to write. But as each day passed, her belief in her parents' safety became more frail and the reality that she might never see them again ended her childhood. She was fourteen years old. She had to be responsible for herself.

She then decided to follow her earlier ambition to become a kindergarten teacher. In order to obtain a credential to teach kindergarten in Switzerland, Karola first had to have a household diploma. To get this diploma Karola went to the village each day for two years and learned how to be a good maid.

She learned the proper way to iron a shirt, air bedding, clean, and cook. To this day, she can mend a sweater or garment without a stitch showing. During this time, she was also responsible for housework at the home. At the end of two years, she passed her finals and received her household diploma. Her next step was to get a teaching credential. Karola hoped that when she got to Palestine, she could become a kindergarten teacher in the children's house. The children's house was a separate building where all the children of a kibbutz lived. When a baby was one month old, it went to the children's house where it was cared for and taught by nurses and teachers. Parents were allowed to visit their child for two hours each day.

Sometimes Karola thought her whole world revolved around "when." When she got her household diploma, when she received her teaching degree, when she could leave the home.

For over six years, Karola had dreamed about the day the war would be over. She had even written an essay about it. In the essay she described the shouting and laughing—the eager anticipation of reunions with families, the packing of belongings, the tearful good-byes to fellow refugees, and the trip to Geneva to catch the train home . . . .

On May 7, 1945, the war in Europe was truly over. There was relief and gladness but no shouting and laughing. Instead, Wartheim lived up to its meaning, "waiting home." Wait to find out where each of them would go. Wait for papers. And most importantly, wait for news of their relatives and friends. Had they survived the Holocaust?

Each week the director at the home received a roster from the Red Cross that listed the names of the people who had survived the concentration camps. Each week the director called the young people together and read the list of names. Each week Karola crossed her fingers, held her breath, and prayed. Each week her hopes of seeing her family again diminished. The six months that she had expected to be separated from her family had now stretched into more than six years. And now she knew the separation was forever. The void in her heart could never be filled.

Very soon, the home would no longer have a place for refugees. Karola realized she had to take charge of her life herself.

After she had received her household degree, she had applied and been accepted by Sonnegg, a kindergarten-teacher academy. The school was located in the town of Ebnat-Kappel which is in the eastern part of Switzerland. Karola was eager to begin classes. The Swiss Aid Committee for Refugee Children, which had helped Jewish refugee children previously, agreed to pay her tuition and to give her ten francs for spending money each month. This was especially exciting to Karola because she had never had any money in all her seventeen years, but at the same time she was concerned because she knew that once she received a diploma from the academy, she would have to leave Switzerland. Where would she go? She was not only homeless but countryless.

In spite of the lure of money of her own and a teaching credential, the challenge and comradeship of Zionism appealed to her idealism and her need for identity. She chose to go to Palestine with the Zionist organization to build a future for herself and others so that never again would her people be homeless and unwanted. And perhaps, helping immigrants in Palestine who had survived the concentration camps would ease the pain of her own loss.

7

Changes

Because Karola talked so fervently about the Zionist organization and Palestine, most of the fifty or so young people remaining at the home signed up to emigrate with her. By July 7, 1945, two months after the end of the war in Europe, the refugees had all left Wartheim.

The Zionists said that the young people would need nothing more in Palestine than a knapsack to pack their old clothes. In their new country, everything would be provided—food, shelter, appropriate clothing.

The Zionist representatives also advised them that they had a choice to make once they arrived in Palestine. They could join the Youth Alliyah and work half a day and study half a day or they could be members of the Chalutzim and work the entire day. Totally swept up in the Zionist cause, Karola chose to belong to the Chalutzim. She figured that the struggling country needed full-time workers.

Since Karola and the others had no passports or were not citizens of any country, an international group gave each of them a special document called a Nansen passport. This type of passport was first issued after World War I and served as an international identity certificate for displaced persons.

After leaving Wartheim, the young people went to the Swiss town of Bex. They spent several months there studying Hebrew and learning more about Palestine and Zionism.

Karola, who had been so enthusiastic about emigrating to Palestine, now felt unsure of her decision. After all, she had been at Wartheim for over six years. Although she had, at times, thought the orphanage was like a prison, still she had been safe. Now, once again, she was leaving the familiar for the unknown. Had she been wise to embrace Zionism without knowing anything about its past? Did she really want to be a Zionist and trade her privacy and her desire to live as she chose for a life in a collective? Even though she lived in Bex with 120 young people with a common goal, she still felt alone and unsure.

And like any teenage girl, she longed for a boyfriend—someone who thought she was special. Along with her doubts about Palestine were doubts about herself. Would anyone ever love her—someone so short, so ugly? Her feelings of inadequacy are reflected in her diary entries scattered throughout *All in a Lifetime.*

Of course, there was Franz, one of the older German Jewish Kinder Transport children who had spent his time at Basel, Switzerland. But, though Franz was attracted to Karola, she was enchanted with Michael, a Polish Jew who with his family had escaped from Poland and the Nazis. The family first went to Belgium only to discover that the Nazis had taken control of that country, too. Undaunted, Michael and his sister fled Belgium and headed by foot south toward Switzerland. They crossed the Alps and were taken in by a Swiss family. For a time Michael had worked as a waiter, and later he became a Zionist organizer.

To sort out her concerns about Zionism and Michael and her doubts about herself, Karola decided to go to Zurich for a brief holiday. She needed to be by herself, lost in the crowds of the Swiss city. She wanted time to reevaluate her goals. And she yearned to once again enjoy being an ordinary, middle-class individual.

The last evening in Zurich she spent with Franz. They rented a boat and rowed around Lake Zurich. The sky was star-studded. Lights from the city cast their neon reflections on the clear water. Karola and Franz talked, and she realized that Franz was not only a responsive listener but that he understood her uncertainties. It helped to share her doubts and realize that Franz too had concerns.

In the almost two months she had been in Bex her uncertainties had not diminished. She wanted to be a part of communal living; she wanted to help other refugees—to give them love and understanding; she wanted purpose in her life. But most of all, she wanted to belong, to be liked by the other Zionists. Never an overly confident person, Karola was plagued by self-doubt. Was she the only one among the refugees who had doubts and questions? Like many teenagers, she was sure that everyone hated her. She wondered if she was meant to live in a commune.

Finally the two months of learning and training in Bex were over. The day before the youngsters were to leave for Palestine, they took a train to Geneva for a farewell party given by the Swiss people who had been involved with the Kinder Transport children for the past seven years.

Karola was chosen to make a speech on behalf of the children. She told the audience about how thankful they all were that Switzerland had taken them in. She said that without the Kinder Transport most and perhaps all of the refugees present would have been tortured in a German concentration camp or have lost their lives.

She didn't tell them that she thought the Swiss people could have shown more affection to the homeless children. Nor did she say how much the refugees resented being treated like servants by the Swiss Jewish children who came to Wartheim, or how cruel the

Swiss were in not allowing other refugees into their country, thus virtually sentencing them to death.

The day after the farewell party the refugees headed for the train station in Basel for their long trip to Marseilles, France. Michael said that they would spend a couple of days there before traveling to Toulon where they would board the ship for Palestine.

Michael. Karola was still infatuated with him. He was only two or three years older than she, but he seemed so adult and worldly. The others in the group thought he was special, too.

The refugees had packed their meager possessions into their knapsacks. A few of them also had suitcases. Time and again, Michael had assured them they wouldn't need anything more once they got to Palestine.

Just before they were to board the train, Michael asked Karola if she would do him a favor. Would she! Of course. He asked that she bring him something from his knapsack. When she asked what to look for, he said she'd know when she found it.

She ran to where the knapsacks were stashed, ready to be carried aboard the train, and quickly found Michael's pack. She rummaged through his belongings—socks, underwear, pants—and then she found it. A gun.

Horrified, she hurried back to him. When she asked Michael for an explanation, he said that the gun was his father's, and he was taking it to Palestine strictly as a souvenir. In a low voice, Michael asked if Karola would be responsible for it.

She looked at the gun. So dangerous and deadly. She glanced up at Michael. So handsome and mature. There was no contest. Of course she'd carry the weapon. For Michael, the gun was a memento of his father. She knew how important souvenirs from loved ones were.

Michael explained why he couldn't carry the holstered gun. He said the British would be overseeing their ship to Palestine. They would search the men in the group, but because the British officials were very gentlemanly, they probably wouldn't bother a young girl.

Later, after they arrived in Palestine, Michael admitted that the gun wasn't a souvenir from his father. Michael had wanted the weapon smuggled into Palestine for the Haganah, the Jewish underground army. As an adult, Karola realized that outrageous acts are committed sometimes for a particular cause. But at the time, she was dismayed at Michael's thoughtless act. If the British had discovered the gun on her, the entire group of refugees could have been barred from entering Palestine. Fortunately, she was not searched.

The train ride to Marseilles, France, was a long, tedious journey. As Karola passed through villages and stations, she saw the remnants of the war everywhere. Countless buildings lay in heaps of rubble. Many of the railroad station houses had been burned to the ground. Even some of the fields had gaping holes in them where bombs had exploded.

Still, Karola looked forward to meeting the people in her new homeland of Palestine. And Palestine was located on the Mediterranean Sea! She envisioned deep blue water washing upon beaches with sand as white and fine as salt.

When the emigrants arrived in Marseilles, they were taken to the beach where tents had been set up for them. They were there for two cool nights—two nights in which Karola cuddled for warmth and solace in Franz's arms.

From Marseilles they took a train to Toulon. Karola was one of the 600 refugees authorized to board the ship. On the shore another 600 people hoping to emigrate to Palestine, waited. Since they did not have the necessary immigration papers, there was little chance that they would be permitted to board.

This was because after World War I, the Turkish Empire, which included Palestine, was dismembered. The League of Nations then placed Palestine under British rule. In the ensuing years, the British faced a constant balancing act in their efforts to be fair to the Arab nationalists who had lived in Palestine for many years and the Jews who thought of Palestine as their rightful homeland. (The Jews had fled from Palestine some 1,800 years previously when the Romans occupied their country.) As the Zionist movement, which was a political movement and not a religious one, grew in strength, the hostility between the Arabs and the Jews increased. The persecution of the Jews by the Hitler regime strengthened the Zionists' belief that the Jews should have their own state. After the war, many of the Jews were homeless. The Zionists encouraged them to come to Palestine—to come home. But the British, in an effort to maintain a fair ratio of Jewish settlers and Arab nationalists, allowed only a certain number of Jewish refugees into Palestine.

The reason for this policy was that on November 2, 1917, British Lord Arthur James Balfour stated that the British government favored the establishment in Palestine of a national home for the Jewish people. Britain would do all it could to facilitate the achievement of that object. The policy also stated that nothing should be done that might prejudice the civil and religious rights of existing non-Jewish communities in Palestine.

Karola's group of emigrants all had the proper documentation to board the ship. When Michael was told by one of his Zionist superiors to get the 600 people waiting on shore on the ship, Michael, the master manipulator, saw that the British official who checked the passengers' immigration papers wasn't very thorough. After Karola and her group boarded, Michael gathered up their papers. He told the immigration official that he had left something on shore. Once on shore, he handed out the immigration records to the 600 people, who then boarded the ship with the "borrowed" but necessary papers.

The additional passengers created overcrowding, and food that was to have served 600 passengers now had to be stretched to feed 1200 people. Karola and some of the other refugees gave up their cabins for the mothers and children. Karola, nestled in Franz's arms, slept on the deck under starry skies. For Karola, the six-day trip was mostly an adventure filled with folk dancing and the singing of Hebrew songs. But in moments of solitude she wondered what lay ahead. Would she be happy living and working in a commune? Would she feel fulfilled or disappointed? Would she ever see Europe again?

She consoled herself with thoughts of ocean waves, one after another, cresting and breaking as they washed up, foamy and spent, on the Palestinian shore. There would be work—demanding but rewarding work—but work in a breathtaking setting.

In mid-afternoon the ship docked in Haifa. Haifa was everything Karola expected, with its beautiful bay and the city itself, so white and gleaming, built on the slopes of Mount Carmel. She could

Like these Jewish refugees, Karola entered Palestine by ship at the port of Haifa.

hardly wait to walk along the waterfront, to watch the waves peak and fall, to feel the gentle sea breeze.

The refugees didn't linger in Haifa, but were transported to Camp Atlit, which was about ten miles from the city. Again, as they had in Switzerland, the refugees put in waiting time while the British checked their papers. Fortunately, no one was prohibited from staying in Palestine—not even the 600 people with the "borrowed" immigration papers. Karola wondered if Michael had once again outsmarted the British. Or perhaps, once immigrants were actually in Palestine, the British didn't deport them.

The camp, enclosed in barbed wire, unnerved Karola with its similarities to photographs she had seen of concentration camps. Had her family been in a camp like this? Her thoughts were haunted by visions of her father, mother, and grandmother standing behind the barbed wire fence of a concentration camp as they awaited their grisly and certain deaths.

The similarities between pictures of concentration camps and Camp Atlit was even more apparent when Uncle Lothar, her mother's brother, came to see her. Because of the barbed wire fence surrounding Camp Atlit, Karola could only touch fingers with Uncle Lothar. But they talked. For the first time in seven years, Karola visited with a member of her family.

Uncle Lothar had left Germany and gone to Palestine before the war began. Now, he was settled in a well-established, wealthy kibbutz called Ashdot Yaakov. He invited Karola to live in the same settlement. His offer certainly had appeal. At Uncle Lothar's kibbutz she would have a relative who knew the workings of collective living. She probably even could further her education. And she would be close to a family member. Although Uncle Lothar's offer certainly attracted Karola, she had already made plans to go to a different kibbutz with the other refugees.

Several days later, Karola and about thirty-five of the other new immigrants left the camp and headed for their kibbutz, which was called Ayanot. The truck ride was bumpy and hot. Karola looked out the rear of the truck bed to a barren land. There were no trees or greenery—just the relentless hot sun in a clear blue sky beating down on the dry land. Hardly a seascape. And such a change from Switzerland!

When they reached Ayanot, which wasn't too distant from Haifa, Karola was surprised at how pretty the settlement was, with its white stucco buildings, lush green lawns, and many trees.

Ayanot was home to about 300 people. It was mainly an agricultural kibbutz. There were olive groves, grape vineyards, apple orchards, and orange and grapefruit groves. Seeing the cows and chickens on the farmland brought back sweet memories to Karola of her grandparents' place in Wiesenfeld.

But from the time the German Jewish immigrants arrived at Ayanot, the Polish Jews who had settled Ayanot resented them. Karola remembered how in Switzerland the Swiss Jews had treated them like servants and now, here in Palestine, the Polish Jews showed the same scornful behavior toward the newcomers.

In a way, Karola thought, the whole Jewish resentment had come full circle. When she was growing up in Germany, the German Jews looked down on the Polish Jews because they seemingly lacked the culture and refinement the German Jews had. In Switzerland, the tables were turned. The Swiss considered the German Jewish refugees as second-class people. Now, the circle was complete with the Polish Jews looking down on the German Jewish emigrants. It was as though the Polish Jews blamed them for not being smart enough to get out of Germany before the atrocities began, as they had.

The Polish Jews resented anything German. Immediately they demanded that any of the immigrants with German-sounding names change them to Hebrew ones. Karola took her middle name Ruth. She kept the initial K. She believed that by using her middle name as her given name and keeping the initial K for Karola as her middle name, her family would be able to find her.

Although intellectually she believed her family members were dead because their names never appeared on any Red Cross survivor lists, still, deep within her, she harbored a hope. To admit to herself that they were dead was too harsh a reality.

8

Kibbutz Living

Ruth (as Karola was now known) settled into communal living and gradually learned more about the kibbutz movement. The movement had begun in 1909 when some young Jews left their homes in Russia to live in the Holy Land, or Palestine. The Russian Jews wanted to establish a community in the new land where everything was shared by its members. The settlement would be a haven where neither money nor position would be a measure of an individual's worth.

The first such community was the Degania kibbutz, which was built south of the Sea of Galilee and overlooked the route to Galilee and Haifa. But when the Russian Jews arrived in Palestine, they discovered that the land they had intended to farm had been neglected for centuries. Before they could plant, they had to drain swamps, correct erosion problems, and anchor the dunes so that the winds would not blow the sandy soil onto the cultivated fields. Reclaiming the land was a slow process. But with dedication and hard work, the newcomers not only succeeded in producing crops but also in fulfilling their dream of a people living together in a share-and-share-alike community. Other kibbutzim were soon established.

Ruth learned that in some of the kibbutzim the people were comfortably well-off, while in others the people were poor and struggled just to exist. But regardless of whether a kibbutz was wealthy or poor, the system of government was the same.

Every kibbutz was governed by a series of committees that were responsible for certain phases of the community life, such as financial and economic planning, education, culture, and child care. Once a year all the members of the kibbutz gathered together for a general meeting. At this annual gathering they discussed and developed the policies for the next year and elected new officers to the governing committees. Any grievances of the past year were aired and resolved by the entire kibbutz membership.

Freed from household responsibilities, the women worked alongside the men. Some of the women worked in the fields while others cooked for the entire community or cleaned communal property. The men and women ate in a common dining hall. And the children were well cared for in the kibbutz's House of Children. The children of the commune fared much better than the adults because the youngsters represented the future.

No one was forced to remain in a particular kibbutz but was at liberty to move to another. And if someone wished to leave communal living entirely, he or she was free to do so. There were no wages paid to the workers, but once a year money was given to each member for a two-week vacation.

In Ruth's kibbutz there were a few residential buildings, each divided into four rooms. Several of the buildings were nicer, with bathrooms for each section, but many of the residences were not much more than shacks with corrugated tin roofs. The communal facilities, such as the dining hall, the children's center, and the meeting hall, were all much more pleasing and comfortable than the individual living quarters for the residents.

Ruth elected to live in one of the few tents that were available. She shared this canvas home with three young men. Since no one was allowed personal possessions, the space in the tent was ample for the four cots with straw mattresses and the two changes of clothing issued to the kibbutz members.

There were no sidewalks connecting the various buildings. When it rained, Ruth avoided the mud by jumping from one asphalt square to another.

Daily life in the kibbutz was drudgery. And the resentment that the regular kibbutz members had toward the newly arrived refugees was apparent in their treatment of them. The better housing was reserved for the original members of the kibbutz. Although a girl from the established membership was assigned by the kibbutz officials to be an adviser of sorts to Ruth's group, the girl paid little or no attention to the newcomers. As a result, the refugees banded together, as they had in the Swiss orphanage, to support and comfort each other.

The regular kibbutz members' hostility was also evident in their method of assigning work details. The menial tasks always went to Ruth's group. At first, Ruth worked her eight-hour shift in the fields picking tomatoes and olives, but later she was assigned the job of cleaning the toilets and attending to other household chores. She longed to be an assistant to the kindergarten teacher. After all, she had wanted to pursue a teaching career in Switzerland but had given up that opportunity to emigrate to Palestine. Why couldn't she seek that goal here?

Day after day, Ruth spent in hard labor. Night after night, she filled her diary with self-doubts. She longed for her parents. How had they died? Where were they buried? She was seventeen years old and was this all there was to life? Why was she so short and ugly? She had a duty to work for the future of Palestine. But when would her chance for a future of her own come? She was so ignorant. How could she ever hope to hold the interest of a man?

And Michael. She had to put him out of her mind and heart. She just had to.

Today, Ruth feels that someone within the kibbutz should have shown some compassion and guided the young refugees. But instead of recognizing the young people's need for education and making certain they attended the commune's high school, the kibbutz membership used the newcomers' zeal and enthusiasm for their own purposes—for the development and expansion of the commune. Many of the regular kibbutz members were older and unable to labor as hard as the youngsters. Perhaps if these members had shown more concern for the newcomers, the young people would not have been so eager to establish their own kibbutz or move to another as they eventually felt forced to do.

Still, Ruth's life was not all dreary. She enjoyed swimming at a nearby kibbutz. And sometimes there were movies. At every opportunity she visited her Uncle Lothar at his commune, just two hours away, and was thrilled when he turned over his kibbutz's yearly allotment of one book to her. Although Michael hovered in her heart, he was still unattainable. Ruth enjoyed the attention of several boyfriends, like Dror (Franz's new Hebrew name) Shaul, (one of her tentmates), and Shaul's soldier brother, Kalman. On Friday nights there was folk dancing to the music of an accordion or a harmonica.

Although there was a synagogue in the settlement, Ruth did not attend services. People worked on Saturday since the kibbutz was not Orthodox. For them at the kibbutz, holidays like Passover were not cause for a religious celebration commemorating the Israelites being allowed to leave Egypt as described in the Book of Exodus. People of the kibbutz celebrated Passover because of a bountiful harvest. But out of respect for her parents, Ruth continued to fast on special Jewish days.

Another change for Ruth was people's liberal attitude concerning sex. Members of the kibbutz wanted the young people to know each other, get married, and produce children for the good of Palestine. So, young boys and girls were encouraged to room together in the hope that they would marry.

Eighteen-year-old Ruth wasn't ready at this time for such a relationship. She had come to Palestine eager to do her part in building a home for the Jews. But certain aspects of commune living had disillusioned her. Although she thought collective living was a good way to build a community, she knew now that the promise of equal work and equal benefits for all was not always the case. Some of the people in the commune did not do their share of the work.

Another thing that bothered her about communal living was the lack of family life. A month after a baby was born, the infant was placed in the House of Children, and the mother, women being

Jewish settlers dancing the "hora" in a new kibbutz.

equal with men, was freed to work, unburdened with child care. Parents could visit their child at the House of Children for several hours after finishing their work for the day.

In a *McCall's* article, written by Barbara Grizzuti Harrison in 1983, Ruth is quoted as saying, "Raising children communally does not work. What we see in Israel today is that everyone wants their children in their homes." She believes that the nuclear family is in Israel to stay.

Certainly it is understandable why Ruth would object to children being reared communally. From the time she was ten years old, she had experienced institutionalized living. Now, she yearned for privacy, for an opportunity to pursue her own goals, and for family living.

At the end of her first year in Palestine, Ruth took her two-week vacation and stayed with Uncle Lothar. When she returned to her commune, many of her fellow refugees had left to go to other kibbutzim. At first, Ruth was hurt that they had departed without her, but then she realized that there were no telephones, no way to contact her. When the opportunity to leave arose, they had to go immediately.

Ruth decided that it was time for her to relinquish her membership in a kibbutz too. Late in 1946, she moved to another commune named Yagur. This settlement was closer to Haifa. More importantly, it had a school for those wishing to become kindergarten teachers. Since Ruth was no longer a member of a kibbutz, she had to pay tuition at the Yagur kibbutz school. She agreed to work in the school's kitchen for one year in exchange for the next year's enrollment. To get a kindergarten teacher credential took three years. By working one year and going to school the next, it would take six years for Ruth to obtain a teaching credential.

For the next year, Ruth worked in the school's kitchen. She didn't wait for her education to start but began studying Hebrew again on her own. Some new friends tutored her in French and math.

At the end of the year, she realized that her plan of work a year, attend school a year, wasn't practical.

Ruth also visited a distant relative of her mother, named Liesel, who lived in Jerusalem. Liesel introduced Ruth to her friends, Mr. and Mrs. Goldberg, who were wonderful, caring people. Because of Mrs. Goldberg's social position and connections, Ruth was granted a scholarship at a seminary in Jerusalem to pursue her goal of becoming a kindergarten teacher.

Again, Ruth packed her meager belongings and moved into a residence for young women in Jerusalem. The residence was similar to a youth hostel or the YWCA. For the first time in her nineteen years, Ruth had a room to herself.

While she waited for her classes to begin, Ruth worked as a waitress and baby-sitter. She didn't keep the job of waitressing long because she was too generous in filling the cups of coffee, even though she had been warned to fill them only three-quarters full.

Her baby-sitting jobs demanded much of her energy. Parents expected Ruth not only to care for the young ones but when the children went to bed, she also was expected to keep herself busy by sewing, washing dishes, or ironing. And, unlike modern parents in the United States, the parents in Jerusalem left no soft drinks or treats for the baby-sitter.

Still, Ruth was happy to be in a city again, and Jerusalem was fascinating to her. There is a Jewish legend that says Jerusalem is the cornerstone of the whole earth. It is a holy place for three great religions. The Jews have held Jerusalem in their hearts for five thousand years. Wherever Passover was celebrated, the words, "Next year in Jerusalem," were said. The Christians have cherished Jerusalem for almost two thousand years. And it has been a sacred city for the Muslims for some fourteen hundred years.

Ruth wandered through old Jerusalem and marveled at the colorful bazaars, the bustling markets, and the crowded residential districts. She visited the Wailing Wall where the Temple of Solomon once stood.

In new Jerusalem the sound of traffic, the bustling crowds, and the excitement of the city thrilled Ruth. What fun it was to walk along the city streets and look in the store windows.

When her classes at the kindergarten seminary began in April 1947, Ruth quit her daytime job. Again, she felt unsure of herself. Would she be able to keep up with the other students? After all, her classmates had a high school education. Her formal education had ended with the eighth grade. She was not surprised at how difficult the studies proved to be.

Part of her problem was lack of money. Her scholarship, which had been arranged by Mrs. Goldberg, only covered seminary expenses. So when classes were over for the day, she again worked

Ruth wandered through the ancient section, or "old city," of Jerusalem.

as a baby-sitter. This left little time for studying. Still, she perse-
vered.

Then one day Ruth was visited by a Mrs. Nettie Sutro. Mrs.
Sutro had been in charge of the Swiss agency that handled the
arrangements for some of the refugees to be taken care of in
Wartheim. Mrs. Sutro explained that since the agency was no longer
functioning, she was distributing the money left over from its
operating fund to the children who had been cared for at Wartheim.
There was enough remaining money for each child to receive 2000
Swiss francs, which was equivalent to about 500 dollars.

This gift certainly alleviated the money situation for Ruth.
Instead of just window-shopping, now she would be able for the
first time in her life to buy some clothes.

But, even achieving her goal of attending school, receiving the
unexpected money, and having her distant relative, Liesel, also
living in Jerusalem, did not make up for Ruth's lack of family life.
Often, she wandered the city streets on a Friday night just to see
the Sabbath candles glowing in the windows. And she remembered
Friday nights in Frankfurt so long ago and going to the synagogue
with Father while Mother stayed home to prepare the dinner and
light the candles. Would she ever be part of a family again?

9

A New Life

Although the British tried to maintain peace in Palestine, the tension between the Arabs and the Jews steadily mounted. Jewish soldiers destroyed an Arab village. The Arabs retaliated by massacring a convoy of Jewish nurses and doctors. The fight for Palestine injured Arab and Jewish civilians as well as soldiers from both sides. But there was one matter on which the Arabs and Jews agreed. Both wanted the British out of Palestine. And the British, caught as they were in the middle of the growing hostilities, also wanted out.

In April 1947, the British government referred the problem of Palestine to the United Nations, which voted on November 29 to partition the country into Jewish and Arab states. The holy city of Jerusalem was to be a neutral zone under international control.

Britain's control in Palestine would end on May 15, 1948. In the last months of British rule, civil war raged between the Arabs and the Jews. The Arabs attacked isolated kibbutzim. The Jews sabotaged Arab convoys and ambushed Arab camps. Each side committed atrocities.

In Jerusalem, the sound of bombs exploding and machine guns firing echoed throughout the city. First, the Arabs controlled several blocks of the holy city, and then the Jews recaptured the area.

The Haganah, the Jewish underground army, urged civilians, the prime targets for Arab attacks, to volunteer for army service. Ruth enlisted in the Haganah because, in spite of some disillusionment with the Zionists, she believed that every citizen should participate in some way in defending the Jewish people. She continued with her studies at the teachers' seminary while she underwent basic training in the army.

The army taught her how to dismantle machine guns and reassemble them. The army also taught her how to handle hand grenades. She learned how to shoot and surprised herself at her accurate marksmanship.

After she completed her basic training, Ruth often served as a messenger for the Haganah. The reason for this assignment, she thought, was due to her shortness of stature. She wasn't as noticeable as a tall, lanky individual.

Sometimes, dressed in army khakis, she guarded a rooftop. With a machine gun slung over her shoulder and hand grenades hanging from her belt, she overlooked a checkpoint where the Israeli soldiers inspected each automobile before it entered the city. If the occupant of the car did not know the password, Ruth phoned the proper officials for help. She was authorized to shoot if necessary. Fortunately, she never had to use her weapons.

At 9:00 A.M., May 14, 1948, Sir Alan Cunningham, the last British High Commissioner in Palestine, left Haifa. That same day the Jewish National Council and the General Zionist Council met at Tel Aviv and proclaimed the state of Israel. At 4:00 P.M. in Tel Aviv, David Ben-Gurion, the newly appointed prime minister of the provisional government, made the announcement to the Jews that Israel was now their homeland.

All over the countryside, the people rejoiced. Crowds danced in the streets of villages and cities. Some wept for joy. In Jerusalem, Ruth, along with some friends, cruised the city in the bed of a truck. Shouting and laughing, they celebrated the good news.

But their joy was to be short-lived. The very same day that Israel became a Jewish state, armies from neighboring Arab states invaded the newborn country. Fighting broke out everywhere. Ruth continued to serve as sentry for the army. This was the first of four wars in which the fledgling nation would be involved. The others took place in 1956, 1967, and 1973.

On June 4, 1948, Ruth celebrated her twentieth birthday. After completing her rooftop duty that morning, she returned to the youth hostel for lunch. No sooner had she entered the building than the sirens sounded. She knew she should go immediately to the basement for

David Ben-Gurion, premier of the newly established Jewish state of Israel, May 14, 1948.

Crowds of happy people celebrating the Jewish state of Israel.

protection against the bombs. But the time spent in the candlelit shelter with its benches lined up against the wall was often long and boring. So Ruth returned to her room to get one of her birthday presents, a Hebrew novel, to help pass the time in the basement. She dashed up the stairs and had just returned to the lobby with her book when an Arab bomb detonated outside the hostel.

The deafening sound blasted her senses, and the next thing she knew, she was sitting on the lobby floor, her back against the crumbling plaster wall. A soldier's body lay sprawled next to her. Then a friend knelt down and began to remove Ruth's shoes. Ruth wondered why the girl would take off her new birthday shoes. The smell of dust from the falling plaster mingled with the smell of death. Sirens blared. People cried. She glanced at her feet, now covered in blood. And Ruth wondered if she were going to die.

At the hospital doctors removed shrapnel that had peppered Ruth's body, with a larger piece lodged in her neck. But the injury to her feet caused the most concern. Shrapnel had torn away the flesh on top of one foot. Countless abrasions marred her feet and ankles. It was several weeks before Ruth, using crutches, left the hospital. Fortunately, she suffered no permanent damage from her injuries and was able to complete her studies.

Ruth received her teaching certificate from the kindergarten seminary in the spring of 1949. Although her Hebrew grammar wasn't the best, she began her first kindergarten teaching job in a town named Eshtaol. This was a small village of Yemenites located about halfway between Jerusalem and Tel Aviv. The Yemenites originally came from Yemen, a state south of Saudi Arabia. During the mid-1940s many of them emigrated to Palestine. In the new country, they established their own villages and practiced many of their ancient traditions and rituals.

Ruth enjoyed her first teaching assignment, and she was fascinated by the Yemenites' different culture. In the Yemen culture women were subservient to the men. Yemenite husbands supported both a young wife and an older one. The mothers came to school with the children and Ruth taught them the basics of good housekeeping. Because the mothers could not just be shown a certain task, Ruth had to guide each mother through the particular job. In her autobiography, Ruth tells how, for instance, she could not just scrub one child as an example, but she had to clean every youngster in the classroom so the mother of each child would know how to wash her own offspring. Such a different and exotic world. To Ruth, the Yemenite culture seemed like a fantastic tale from a storybook. She continued to live in Jerusalem and commute each morning via an hour bus ride to the Yemenite village.

One weekend, she met David, an Israeli soldier from Tel Aviv but assigned to a camp near Jerusalem. The attraction between them was immediate, and shortly after they met they were going steady. According to Ruth in her autobiography, David had several characteristics that Ruth appreciated. He was fun to be with. He was a good dancer. He was a soldier. And he wanted to study to be a doctor. Besides those heartwarming attributes, he was short.

A few months after they met, David proposed marriage to her, and she accepted. Still suffering from self-doubts and limited self-value, Ruth couldn't believe her good fortune. Imagine! Someone wanted to marry her! Now she could start a family of her own plus embrace David's many relatives, her ready-made family.

Ruth was dressed in a short, white dress when she and David were married in November 1950, on the terrace of Liesel's apartment. Uncle Lothar and, of course, Liesel were present and many of David's family.

From the terrace Ruth looked out upon a yard of beautiful, mature trees. The afternoon sky had not a cloud. For Ruth, the only cloud in the perfect day was the absence of her parents and grandparents. How she wished they could have shared this special occasion with her.

After the wedding, Ruth and David moved to Paris, France. Israel had won the war against the Arab League and David had been discharged from the army. The plan was that David's parents would pay his medical school's tuition and Ruth would find a job to pay for their living expenses. Ruth found work in a kindergarten for Jewish children. Since the pupils were from different countries, language was a problem. Many of the boys and girls had parents or relatives who had suffered and died in concentration camps, so the German language was not popular. To communicate with the youngsters, Ruth worked on improving her skills in Yiddish and French.

When, in 1951, Israel put a limit on the amount of money that could be sent out of the country, Ruth and David's financial security suffered. David's parents had been sending money for his school tuition, but with Israel's monetary restriction, Ruth now had to look for additional work to ease their financial worries.

Her second job involved teaching Hebrew to older French Jewish children. This was a change from teaching kindergartners but one which she enjoyed. When school was not in session, she worked at summer camps.

Ruth liked living in Paris and enjoyed its museums and theaters. Often, on her way to work, she walked through the Sorbonne, the University of Paris. She wished she could be a student at the Sorbonne. But with no high school diploma, the idea of attending a university seemed an impossible dream.

Then she learned about a one-year refresher/prerequisite course offered by the university. Students whose studies were interrupted because of the war could, upon passing a test at the end of the year, be admitted to the university. Ruth enrolled in the special program and still worked at her kindergarten job. Of all the subjects she studied, psychology appealed to her the most because it dealt with people and their concerns. All her life she had listened to her friends' problems. And she liked exploring her own thoughts and feelings. Her goal now was to become a clinical psychologist. After studying for a year, she took the test, passed, and was admitted as a student to the Institute of Psychology at the Sorbonne.

Finally, to be a student and to be learning about such people as Sigmund Freud, the Austrian physician and founder of psychoanalysis; Charles Darwin, the British naturalist and originator of the theory of organic evolution; and Carl Gustav Jung, the Swiss psychiatrist who founded the school of analytical psychology, thrilled Ruth. Even though the classes were extremely difficult, she thrived on the challenges of education. She did fail a few math exams and science courses but overall did well in her studies at the university.

But Ruth's married life was not as successful as her university life. David had lost interest in becoming a doctor and planned to return to Israel and pursue his education in Middle Eastern studies. But Ruth wanted to stay in Paris and complete her education at the Sorbonne. She and David seemed to be walking different paths. Ruth and David spent the summer of 1954 together in Israel. In the fall, she returned to Paris and David remained in Israel. The next year, Ruth asked David for a divorce, which was arranged by mail.

Ruth continued her studies at the Sorbonne. She lived in a third-floor room with shared bathroom facilities on the ground floor. Money was scarce but it was scarce for Ruth's student friends, too. In spite of limited funds, Ruth found university life exciting and stimulating. After classes Ruth and her friends went to a cafe and lingered hours over one cup of coffee, talking and laughing, in love with their world.

It was at the cafe that Ruth met and fell in love with Dan, a handsome French Jew. Dan was different from any of the young men Ruth had known previously. He had lived in a kibbutz for a couple of years. He had little family. He seemed uncertain as to what to do with his life, so he hung around cafes, visiting with the university students. He was a rather lost individual, and he did not seem eager to find his way in the world. But Ruth loved him.

Then, out of the blue, the West German government sent Ruth a check in the amount of 5,000 marks, which was about 1,500 American dollars. The money was a means of compensation for victims and their families who had suffered at the hands of the Nazis and especially for those whose education had been interrupted. Although Ruth had vowed never to accept any form of payment from the Germans for their part in war crimes, she couldn't turn down this windfall.

Since she would be returning to Israel to teach kindergarten and a Sorbonne degree would not be of value there, Ruth, on the spur of the moment, decided to use the money to visit the United States. She asked Dan to go with her.

Knowing that every penny counted, Ruth purchased fourth-class tickets, the cheapest fare available, which practically put them in the hold of the ship. With some of the remaining money she bought a suit, shirt, and shoes for Dan and a new dress for herself. Thrilled about the trip to America—the golden land, the land of opportunity, and the land where Shirley Temple lived—Ruth barely slept on the journey. The night before they were to land, she stayed on deck to catch the first view of the Statue of Liberty in the New York harbor.

When Ruth and Dan arrived in New York, friends who had moved from Europe to the United States met them at the dock. Ruth couldn't get over how tall the buildings were. She felt even shorter.

After celebrating the reunion with their friends, Ruth and Dan went to a hotel. The room cost seven dollars per night. If they wanted to stay in America for any length of time, Ruth knew they had to find a cheaper place to stay.

She searched through a German Jewish newspaper for room rentals. In the paper she noticed a full-page promotional ad, placed by the Graduate Faculty of Political and Social Science of the New

New arrivals to America wave to the Statue of Liberty.

School for Social Research. Eagerly Ruth read the school ad. A scholarship to earn a master's degree in sociology was offered to a victim of the Nazi regime. Ruth wasted no time in applying for the scholarship.

She discovered that the teachers at the school were for the most part professors who had left Europe to escape Nazi persecution. Since the teachers spoke either French or German, Ruth knew that her language would not be a problem.

From the German Jewish newspaper she not only learned of the scholarship for the university but found a dollar-a-day room with kitchen privileges.

For a short time, Ruth worked as a maid during the day and at night she attended the university. That summer, she took courses that, when completed, would qualify her for a Bachelor of Arts degree.

Then Dan found each of them jobs at the French Embassy. They did odd jobs like hang pictures, create displays for school children, and handle janitorial duties.

In the fall of 1956, Ruth began a series of classes that, when completed, would earn her a master's degree in psychology. Although she was passing the various courses, Ruth discovered that clinical psychology with its various experiments on rats didn't interest her. She wanted to be involved with people. She changed her major to sociology, which is the study of organized groups of humans within their environment. She narrowed her field of interest to the study of the family, which proved to be the first stepping stone to her future successful career.

10

A Surprising New Career

Besides receiving the university scholarship, Ruth had added cause for happiness. She learned that she was pregnant. Ruth had always believed that because of her smallness, she would not be able to have children. With such exciting and unexpected news, she and Dan decided to marry.

Because of their limited finances, a private hospital was out of the question. Their baby, Miriam, was born at Municipal Hospital in the Bronx. Miriam was a beautiful newborn, and Ruth's self-esteem took a more positive turn. Miriam, to her mother, seemed to grow prettier each day.

Money was scarce in Ruth and Dan's household so only the absolute necessities were purchased for the baby. Fortunately, Ruth, as she had done in the past, had built a network of friends in New York. One of them gave Ruth a complete layette for the baby. Someone else lent her a high chair, and another friend lent Ruth a baby carriage. Ruth was extremely proud of her baby. One day, she pushed the buggy from her apartment to the university, a total of four miles, so that her professors and fellow students could see her beautiful infant.

In 1958, when Miriam was one year old, Dan decided he wanted to return to Europe but Ruth wanted to complete her education before going back to Israel. In addition, Ruth's life brimmed with the excitement of school, the baby, her friends, whereas Dan's life seemed to be in neutral. Together they had very little to talk about. Dan left for France and Ruth continued in her studies. Not too much later, Ruth and Dan divorced and Ruth became the sole supporter of Miriam.

Ruth quit her job at the French Embassy and went to work gathering opinions for a market research company. Her duties consisted of calling people on the telephone and asking what they thought about certain products. At night, she attended classes at the university. The English language was still a "foreign" language for Ruth. People advised her to enroll in a speech class to rid herself of a heavy accent.

She knew she had to learn English, but with work during the day, studies in the evening, and a child to care for, Ruth lacked the time and energy. To teach herself the English language, she bought *True Confession* magazines and read them cover to cover. The stories about people and their problems intrigued her and the writing was simple and clear. A friend gave her a television set, which was fun for Miriam because she liked cartoons and good for Ruth because she could hear English spoken.

Ruth's main concern was making enough money to provide food and shelter for Miriam and herself. Fortunately, there were people and organizations to help her. The Jewish Family Service paid a family to care for Miriam while Ruth worked and went to school. Again, when Miriam was old enough to go to nursery school, the organization provided the funds for her to attend a German Jewish Orthodox nursery school.

Friends handed down their children's outgrown clothes for Miriam; friends baby-sat; and others gave their professional help free of charge. For example, when Miriam fell and hurt herself at school, Ruth took her to a hospital where a doctor friend treated Miriam at no charge and then drove Ruth and Miriam to their apartment.

One day Ruth was notified by the Immigration and Naturalization Service that she had to leave the country within the next twenty-four hours. She was frantic. Twenty-four hours! What country would take her and Miriam? She couldn't go to Germany and Switzerland wouldn't welcome her. She intended to return to Israel but only after she completed her education in America. What could have gone wrong? She had been so careful about filling out the necessary forms and having the proper visa. When she first came to the United States, she had a visitor's visa. Then the French Embassy, where she worked for a time, issued her an embassy visa. Presently, she had a student's visa. A lawyer friend handled the immigration problem and waived the fee.

In spite of long days filled with work, caring for Miriam, and school, Ruth managed to squeeze some recreation with her many friends into her busy schedules. She enjoyed camping with fellow students in upstate New York. Often, Ruth provided the place and the potato chips for a party, and the guests brought the rest of the food and drinks. As the students at the Sorbonne had done, students at the New School for Social Research met at a cafe. For hours, they lingered over a cup of coffee, talking about classes, professors, and world issues.

During this time, an Egyptian named Eddie asked Ruth to marry him. Although he was handsome and very nice, Ruth declined his proposal. She felt that her Jewish heritage was too much a part of her to marry an Egyptian. She also refused a proposal from an Episcopal priest. He thought that in their union, they could unite Judaism and Christianity by her reading the scriptures in Hebrew and his reciting them in English. Ruth refused his proposal, too. Still, she wanted to remarry. She wanted a father for Miriam.

In 1959, Ruth received her master's degree in sociology from the New School of Social Research. Her thesis concerned the 100 German Jewish children who were sent to Switzerland in the Kinder Transport at the beginning of World War II. In doing the research for her thesis, Ruth discovered that all of the young people who participated in the Kinder Transport to Switzerland had gone on to lead successful lives. This made her feel especially proud of her peers.

But in the sociology field, a master's degree was only the first step toward a successful career. Ruth immediately plunged into studying for a doctorate while also working as a research assistant at Columbia University's School for Public Health. Earning an advanced degree required more classes, a dissertation (a long, formal, researched essay), and a written and oral examination. She passed all the written work, but failed twice to pass the oral examination.

Since the oral examination was so important, she was very disappointed, but she was not devastated. She worked. She cared for her child. She enjoyed her friends.

In 1961 Ruth received an invitation to ski in the Catskill mountains. Her date was Hans, a six-foot young man from Holland. The difference in their heights made riding the ski lift almost an impossibility. At the top of the mountain Hans introduced Ruth to the man who was president of the ski club. More important to Ruth than his title was his height. He was short, not more than five-foot-five. For the rest of the day, she shared the ski lift with Manfred Westheimer and they talked all that day and into the wee hours of the morning.

Ruth learned that Fred also had been born in Germany. In 1938, his family moved to Portugal. As the Hitler regime overcame one European country after the next, Fred's parents worried that Portugal might be the next country to be invaded. So in 1941, they shipped their fourteen-year-old son to Kentucky to live with his aunt while they remained in Portugal. After Fred finished high school in Kentucky, he served in the U.S. Army. Later, he graduated in engineering from Pratt Institute and from Polytechnic Institute of Brooklyn. His job at present was chief engineer with a consulting firm.

When Ruth returned from her ski trip to New York, she told her friend Debbie that she had met the man she was going to marry. As Ruth mentions in her autobiography, Fred was not only handsome, he was also intelligent. And he was easy-going. He had a job and a car. He was short and he liked children. Besides all those attributes, he played Jewish folk songs on his harmonica. What more could Ruth ask for in a husband?

On December 10, 1961, nine months after Ruth and Fred met on the ski hill, they were married at the Windemere Hotel in New York City. Many of Ruth's friends attended—quite different from her first marriage to David when Ruth had only Liesel and her Uncle Lothar as her guests. Mathilde, her best friend, who had journeyed to Wartheim with Ruth, came from Germany for the occasion. The day before the wedding, Fred's parents flew in from Portugal.

Up to the time she married, Ruth had always planned to finish her education and then return to Israel to live. But Fred was more American than Zionist. He did not want to leave the United States. And Ruth had to admit that in the five years she had lived in New York, she too had become Americanized.

The newlyweds found an apartment in the Washington Heights section of New York City. In no time at all, they were a family, with Miriam even referring to Fred as "Daddy." A few years later, in 1964, their son Joel was born.

With two children and a household to cope with, Ruth knew she couldn't manage a full-time job. Instead, she worked twenty hours a week as a researcher in the School of Public Health and Administrative Medicine at Columbia University. Her job involved several projects concerning patient care. Probably the most satisfying aspect of the job was Ruth's first publishing credits as coauthor of several scholarly articles pertaining to public health.

In 1965, Ruth became an American citizen. She had been in the United States for six years. In her autobiography Ruth pointed out how proud she was to become a citizen of a country that treated its refugees, such as herself, so generously.

Later, in 1967, when funds were cut off for the public health program at Columbia, Ruth applied for a job at a Planned Parenthood clinic in Harlem and soon became its project director. For three years she spent her days at the clinic. Her job involved training and supervising several dozen women in the method of gathering contraceptive and abortion information from about 2000 women in

Ruth with her husband, Fred Westheimer, and her daughter, Miriam.

96

Harlem. Working at the Planned Parenthood clinic made Ruth believe in the importance of contraception and legalized abortion.

After working at the clinic during the day, Ruth attended Columbia University in the evenings where she took courses in family and sex counseling.

When Joel started school, Ruth decided she would work again toward a doctorate degree and in June of 1970, Ruth received her degree, Doctor of Education, from Columbia University. An amazing feat for a person who had been denied the opportunity to attend high school because those in authority believed she was better suited to be a maid than a student.

Ruth began her teaching career that summer as a guest lecturer in the Secondary and Continuing Education Department at Lehman College in the Bronx. In the fall, she was hired as an associate professor in the department of sex counseling. She taught teachers and prospective teachers how to address the topic of sex education in their classes. Although she had no problem in presenting the material from an educational standpoint, she soon realized that she needed more training in family life and sexuality. There were many questions concerning sex to which she didn't have the answers.

One day Ruth saw a notice that Dr. Helen Singer Kaplan was lecturing at the Ford Foundation. Dr. Kaplan had a training program for sex therapists at Cornell Medical School in New York City and was well known and respected in her field. After hearing Dr. Kaplan's lecture, Ruth, as a visitor not a student, attended Dr. Kaplan's class for training sex therapists for several months. At the end of the semester, she asked Dr. Kaplan if she could sign up as a student in the training program. Ruth wanted to learn more about sex therapy in order to teach her classes at Lehman College better. And she had made a decision. She herself wanted to be a sex therapist.

After two years of training with Dr. Kaplan at Cornell Medical School, Ruth received her certificate, qualifying her to be a psychosexual therapist. She began seeing clients on her own, but still continued to teach at Lehman College. Each summer, she went to Israel to teach.

In 1976, while she was in Israel for her usual summer teaching assignment, she was advised that her job was eliminated at Lehman College because of its financial problems. Fortunately, Ruth found another job at Brooklyn College that she thoroughly enjoyed. Her classes were popular with the students. One of her classes on sexuality of the disabled was the first course on this topic ever offered in the country. She published three scholarly papers that year. Her evaluations from the faculty were excellent. At the end of the second year, she was shocked when the head of the department informed her that she would not be part of the staff the next year. Although the chairman did not have to give her reasons for firing Ruth, she mentioned two vague complaints against Ruth. First, she said that Ruth's examinations were not well prepared and second, Ruth's classes were not needed. Ruth found her reasons difficult to believe since her examinations had never been criticized before. Her classes were very popular and other teachers were hired to teach the same subjects.

Ruth later told an interviewer from *People* magazine that she was hurt by not being rehired. She said, "It made me feel as I did when I got kicked out of Germany. Angry, helpless, rejected. As it turns out, it was my big break."

Her big break came about because Ruth, after receiving her certificate as a sex therapist from Cornell Medical School, had continued to help in Dr. Kaplan's program with the training of other students. When the human sexuality program received a request for a speaker, Ruth volunteered. Uneasy at first because of her accent, her topic, and her inexperience in speaking before an audience, Ruth soon became confident in her ability as a speaker.

When she gave a speech for a broadcasters' organization of community-affairs managers from New York, New Jersey, and

Connecticut, Ruth spoke about the need for more sex education programming. She discussed the issues of unwanted pregnancies, homosexuality, and lack of birth control that often were a result of "sexual illiteracy."

Betty Elam, community affairs manager of New York radio station WYNY-FM, was in the audience. She was fascinated by Ruth's presentation and invited her to be a guest on the NBC affiliate's Sunday morning public affairs show.

Ruth had no sooner finished taping the show when Betty Elam called and asked if she would like her own weekly fifteen-minute radio program. Of course she would. Launched in May of 1980, Ruth's *Sexually Speaking* attracted a large audience. Due to its

Ruth became an excellent public speaker. Here she is shown speaking to the American Society of Newspaper Editors in Washington, D.C.

instant success, *Sexually Speaking* was expanded in the fall of 1981 to a one-hour time slot, and the format was changed to a live, phone-in show. According to an article in the *Current Biography Yearbook 1987,* switchboards at the station were jammed almost immediately upon the show's airing, with over 4,000 listeners wanting to talk with Dr. Westheimer about their sexual problems.

One of the callers had difficulty pronouncing Dr. Westheimer's name. In desperation, the caller shortened the name to "Dr. Ruth." The nickname caught on. Although Dr. Westheimer doesn't object to her shortened name, she never refers to herself as Dr. Ruth. But the media does. In fact, Dr. Westheimer is sometimes referred to as "Grandma Freud" or "Doctor Goodsex."

The *Current Biography Yearbook 1987* quotes from an article in which *Newsweek* credits the show's success to Dr. Ruth Westheimer's "effervescent blend of candor, humor, and common-sense practicality."

By the summer of 1983, Dr. Ruth's show attracted a quarter-million loyal listeners weekly and was top-rated for its time period. No one was more surprised than Ruth by the show's popularity. She insisted that all she was doing on radio was educating. No matter whether she was educating or entertaining, Dr. Ruth was on her way to becoming a celebrity.

11

Dr. Ruth

Ruth was not the only "media therapist" dispensing free advice over the airwaves. More than fifty other advisors throughout the country counseled some twenty-five million listeners weekly. Why was Ruth such an instant success? She believes there are several reasons. First, her German accent lessened all sense of impropriety. Because the subject matter sounded less risqué or titillating spoken by a European woman, people immediately felt at ease talking about their intimate concerns. And, as Dr. Ruth says in a *Ladies Home Journal* article, "I'm not a sex symbol so I'm not threatening."

Also, Ruth used the proper names for the different parts of the body. This lifted Ruth's radio talk-show from a cheap-thrill type of program to a scientific and professional level.

Her method of educating and at the same time entertaining her audience is another reason why Ruth has been so successful. Her sense of humor and zest for life are evident in her talks.

In the *Current Biography Yearbook 1987,* Ruth is quoted as saying that she gives "good information in an entertaining way because that's what a good professor does. It's not therapy; it's basic information. It's good advice. . . . I dispense common sense with a smile, based on good scientific knowledge."

In 1982, in addition to her one-hour radio show, Ruth wrote a monthly magazine column for *Playgirl*. And in 1984, *Sexually Speaking* was syndicated by NBC. Syndication enabled Dr. Ruth to be heard by listeners across the nation. About this time, she joined the professional speakers' circuit and spoke at colleges such as Princeton, Harvard, Cornell University, and the U.S. Military Academy at West Point. With a twinkle in her eye, Dr. Ruth said that she was the shortest instructor that West Point cadets ever had.

Dr. Westheimer veered off into another career direction with the publication of her first book, *Dr. Ruth's Guide to Good Sex*, published by Warner Books in 1983. Since then, she has published several other books—*First Love: A Young People's Guide to Sexual Information, Dr. Ruth's Guide for Married Lovers*, and *Loving Couples*, a saucy sort of marriage manual.

But through all her successes, poignant memories still prowled through her mind—memories of her childhood in Frankfurt.

In 1985, Dr. Westheimer returned to Frankfurt for a visit. She had been there several times since leaving with the Kinder Transport in 1939. But this time she was not going to push away the sad feelings that always enveloped her. This time she would go to her parents' home, her grandparents' farm in Wiesenfeld, the park, the school, the synagogue, the cemetery.

And this time she was returning to Frankfurt as the eminent sex therapist "Dr. Ruth." She was well-known in Frankfurt, because her books had been translated into German and her column was syndicated in several newspapers there. In her autobiography, Dr. Westheimer said that several times interviewers referred to her as a German who lived in America. Dr. Westheimer corrected them immediately and said that she was an American of German Jewish ancestry. Everywhere she went, she was recognized and surrounded by admirers—a heady experience after having been forced to leave Germany against her will some fifty years previously.

She went to her old neighborhood where she had lived for ten happy years. The street, Brahmstrasse, hadn't changed. There was the hospital across the street from her home and the park with its beautiful old chestnut trees. She closed her eyes and remembered riding through the park with her father on his bike—too small to reach the pedals but big enough to learn the multiplication tables.

A few blocks down the street was the old cemetery where Grandma Selma went to visit her husband's grave as well as the

Dr. Ruth promoting her new book, *Dr. Ruth's Guide for Married Lovers.*

Dr. Ruth never lets her lack of height stand in her way.

grave of Paul Ehrlich. Grandma Selma had admired Dr. Ehrlich because once he was offered a big promotion if he would renounce Judaism, and he had refused. Paul Ehrlich was awarded the Nobel prize for medicine in 1908.

A short distance from Ehrlich's grave, Dr. Westheimer saw another tombstone. The inscription indicated this grave was for all the victims of the Nazis who hadn't had proper burial.

She went to the house where she had lived. The people invited her to come in and look around. Dr. Westheimer saw the alcove where she used to sleep and remembered the long hallway where she had roller skated or pushed her doll buggy back and forth. She saw the room where her father stored his notions, the kitchen, and the living room, which had also served as Grandma Selma's bedroom. It was the same house but in a new era.

She took a cab to Wiesenfeld where Grandpa Moses and Grandma Pauline had had their farm. The village now had paved streets but otherwise seemed unchanged. Her grandparents' house was still there, but now another family occupied it. There were still geese on the farm. Dr. Westheimer was sure that the geese must be great-great-great grandchildren of her grandparents' geese.

The beautiful synagogue that her father and she used to attend no longer stood. It had not been rebuilt after being destroyed during the terrifying Kristallnacht—"the night of the broken glass."

Her last stop was the railroad station where she had boarded the train for Switzerland so very long ago. The station had been rebuilt and some of the streets were changed, so nothing looked too familiar to Dr. Westheimer. But it made no difference, because in her mind she could still visualize her mother and Grandma Selma running alongside the train for the final look at their beloved child.

That chapter of her life was over. And the Dr. Ruth chapters were still being written. She returned to New York to resume work on her various projects.

In the spring of 1987, Dr. Ruth sought help from psychoanalyst Dr. Mark Blechner. Dr. Blechner told her she was having difficulties not only recalling memories but also in talking about them. Since at that time Dr. Westheimer was writing her autobiography, *All in a Lifetime,* being able to remember incidents about her young life was essential.

Dr. Ruth has said that many times she has told people to seek help from a physician, a counselor, a psychiatrist, or another professional. But she herself didn't practice what she preached. Even when her children had asked what it was like to be an orphan, she immediately changed the subject. It wasn't until she started writing her autobiography that she realized she, too, needed help.

Dr. Blechner said that Dr. Ruth, like many others from the Holocaust era, had not dealt with her parents' fate realistically. This is common among Holocaust survivors. They hold out hope, even with undeniable evidence to the contrary, that somehow their relatives had survived.

When Dr. Ruth arrived at Dr. Blechner's office, she carried a beat-up valise with her. Inside the bag were the blue composition booklets Karola Siegel had used as her diaries. All the letters from her parents, grandparents, and friends from Frankfurt were tied in bundles along with pieces of memorabilia. Over forty years had gone by since Dr. Ruth had read the diaries and letters. Now she needed to unlock her valise of memories and face them if she expected to finish her autobiography.

Dr. Blechner speaks German and Hebrew fluently. With his guidance she was able to reread the diaries and letters and talk about them in German or Hebrew. Buried deep within her had been an irrational guilt that she had abandoned her family. If she had stayed with her parents, perhaps she could have saved them. She realizes now that she has no reason for such guilt but every reason for admiring her parents who loved her so much they sent her to Switzerland to safety. Still, when Dr. Ruth sees a shower head or a fire sprinkler, the image of the gas chamber looms in her mind, and she thinks that this is how her family died.

She has not made an effort yet to find out when and where her parents died, although evidence points to the concentration camp of Auschwitz. Nor did she register their names in the Holocaust memorial in Israel. Recently, however, her daughter Miriam registered her grandparents in the Holocaust memorial.

Dr. Ruth finished her autobiography, *All in a Lifetime*, and published it in 1987.

12

Dr. Ruth Today

Dr. Westheimer had a brief but financially unsuccessful experience with television in 1982. After her radio programs, speaking engagements, and literary successes, she returned to television in the late summer of 1984 with a nationally televised, thirty-minute show entitled *Good Sex with Dr. Westheimer*. Her program aired nightly except for Sundays and was soon renamed *The Doctor Ruth Show*. Around the same time, her Sunday night radio show, *Sexually Speaking*, was syndicated nationally by NBC. More than sixty stations in the United States and Canada carried her radio show.

The public's enthusiastic response to Dr. Westheimer generated numerous articles about this energetic, straightforward woman. Stories about her appeared in the New York *Daily News*, *The New York Times*, *Newsweek*, *Ladies Home Journal*, *McCalls*, *TV Guide*, *People*, *Christianity Today*, *Rolling Stone*, *Time*, *Life*, *Woman's Day*, *Vogue*, and *National Review*.

Along with the many articles published about her, Dr. Westheimer has appeared as a guest on local New York programs as well as on national shows such as *Nightline* with Ted Koppel, the *CBS Evening News* with Dan Rather, *Late Night*

With David Letterman and Johnny Carson's *Tonight Show*. In addition to guest appearances, Dr. Ruth filmed commercials, endorsing products such as typewriters, chocolate mousse, a department store, and soft drinks. Filming these various commercials earned Dr. Ruth another nickname. Because she seemed to have an instinctive sense of what to do in front of a camera, she was called "one-take Westheimer."

Recently, in a special advertising section of *Time* magazine, Dr. Westheimer wrote a humorous spoof on how she would improve the love life of Bugs Bunny, the cartoon character. And perhaps her willingness to spoof and enjoy the unsophisticated things of life

Dr. Ruth, known to some as "one-take" Westheimer, has endorsed many products. Here she appears at a party with the "California Raisins."

110

also contributes to her popularity. Whatever Dr. Ruth does, she does with wholehearted enthusiasm.

Dr. Ruth undertook many other interesting activities in the 1980s—leading a tour of India's "ancient sensual sites," for instance. In 1986, she went to Kenya and Tanzania as part of the Robin Leach television show, *Lifestyles of the Rich and Famous*. Later, she again joined Robin Leach's program and journeyed to China.

Also in 1986 she traveled to Sun Valley, Idaho, to help commemorate its fiftieth anniversary as America's oldest ski resort. While at Sun Valley, she gave psychological coaching to celebrities who were entered in a downhill race. In appreciation for her participation, she was made an honorary Sun Valley ski instructor. Ruth herself is a fine skier, having learned when she lived in Switzerland.

Ruth's career branched off in still another direction in 1986. She made her debut as an actress in the film, *One Woman or Two*, which starred Gerard Dépardieu and Sigourney Weaver and was filmed in Paris, France. One scene in the movie was filmed in a lecture hall of the Sorbonne. Memories of her student life at the Sorbonne replayed in her mind and heart. She remembered well her cold-water flat located on the third floor of an apartment building a few blocks from the school.

Although the movie was not a major success financially or critically, the National Society of Theater Owners bestowed their Star of Tomorrow award upon Ruth as their choice of the year's most promising newcomer to the screen. Ruth knew that the award was a distinct honor. After all, Dustin Hoffman had once been a winner.

Although Dr. Ruth's track record might indicate that she's willing to try anything, she is selective in her commercial choices. She refuses any proposals or ideas that appear to be in poor taste. For instance, she did not want Dr. Ruth dolls marketed, nor did she want to franchise Dr. Ruth Therapy Clinics across the nation. She refused to have a Dr. Ruth telephone line with a prerecorded

Dr. Ruth has traveled all over the world.

message for people who called. And she said no to Dr. Ruth popcorn.

Ruth thinks of herself as an "old-fashioned square." She is a firm believer in marriage and family. Although she supports legalized abortions, she believes that some organizations push abortions. In an article, published in *McCall's* magazine, Ruth says, "I get very, very angry when I think abortion is being offered as a means of birth control. Abortion is a *big deal.* No one who has given birth can dispute that."

Dr. Ruth has strong beliefs in areas other than abortion. For instance, she refuses in her private practice to treat anyone who for pleasure indulges in sexual sadism or cruelty by either physical

Dr. Ruth, Gloria Steinem, and Marlo Thomas together to launch a fundraiser benefitting the *Ms.* Foundation for Women, which supports women's and children's organizations across the country.

113

abuse or mental humiliation. Incest, a sexual relationship between closely related individuals, is another taboo in Dr. Ruth's practice. She objects strenuously to pornography involving children or young people. And she does not condone "joyful promiscuous" behavior. Dr. Ruth believes that joyful and promiscuous are words that cancel out each other. She says, "Going to a bar every night to pick someone up . . . That's desperation, not joy."

Dr. Ruth also believes that each person should follow his or her own religious beliefs in relationships. She urges young people not to be pressured into doing something they don't want to do.

She is a strong advocate of sex education, contraception, and legalized abortion. Her views have aroused some hostility among her critics. For instance, Father Edwin O'Brien, former secretary to Cardinal Terence Cooke is quoted in the *Current Biography Yearbook 1987* as saying, "Her message is just indulge yourself. . . . There's no higher law or overriding morality and there's no responsibility." Other critics claim that Dr. Ruth Westheimer's approach to human problems is like a mother's cure-all, that is, "hot chicken soup." It feels good but doesn't cure anything. Dr. Benjamin Saddock, a New York psychiatrist, calls her radio show "voyeurism of the ear" or, a means of obtaining sexual pleasure from hearing it discussed. Others claim that Ruth is more an entertainer than a psychologist. To back up their claim, they point to the Dr. Ruth tee shirt, a promotional gimmick advertising her radio program on WYNY-FM. In a *Ladies Home Journal* article by Patricia Bosworth, a colleague of Dr. Ruth's comments about the tee shirts. She said that the tee shirt idea was ridiculous, tacky. She added, "You have to be one thing or the other, or the public won't take you seriously. Ruth is trying to have it both ways."

To those critics who accuse her of concentrating on the physical aspect of sex, Ruth is quick to point out that she often talks of relationships. In an article in *Current Biography Yearbook 1987,*

Ruth is quoted as saying, "Sex is not just intercourse. Sex is a smile, sex is holding hands, sex is a relationship."

In the *Ladies Home Journal* article, several colleagues are mentioned who staunchly support Ruth and her talk shows. For instance, Dr. Helen Singer Kaplan, the renowned sex therapist at Cornell Medical School in New York, admires Dr. Ruth's ability to take complex technical information and reword it into practical, understandable advice. She says that Dr. Ruth is not only a good lecturer, but she is warm and caring about people."

Dr. Ruth's former mentor, David Goslin, Ph.D., an executive director with the National Research Council of the National Academy of Sciences in Washington, D.C., believes Ruth has taken a sometimes delicate and potentially dangerous subject and handled it with great skill.

She has a cult following as well as fans from unexpected quarters. Rabbis and sometimes priests praise her candor. According to Barbara Grizzuti Harrison's *McCall's* article, one priest, after Dr. Ruth had talked to his group wrote to her, "We have gained a better insight into the complex and beautiful dimension of our sexual lives and we appreciate your willingness to share your wisdom with us."

Success has not changed Dr. Ruth to any great degree. She still has the same friends among her professional colleagues and former students as she had when she first lectured to a group of New York broadcasters. That lecture launched her career. Her Kinder Transport companions remain close to her, though many live in different parts of the world. She keeps in touch with other long-time friends from the kibbutz in Israel and the Sorbonne in France.

She even stays in contact with her first husband, David. In her autobiography, *All in a Lifetime,* Dr. Westheimer tells that when she and her husband Fred visit in Israel, they occasionally spend time with David, who works for the Israeli government in the finance department. Fred and David seem to respect each other and always share the same joke. Fred asks David why he didn't keep her (Dr. Westheimer), and David always says he's glad Fred has her. Dr. Ruth believes in the adage "to have a friend, be a friend" and has added to that wise saying, "and keep a friend."

She continues to enjoy the same kinds of recreation as she has for many years, like skiing and dining out. She especially enjoys time spent at her country house near Peekskill, New York.

She and Fred still live in the same apartment in a German Jewish neighborhood in New York City's Washington Heights section as they did when they were married almost thirty years ago. The apartment is cluttered but cozy, with an upright piano, ski equipment, magazines and books, photographs, plants, various figurines, a doll collection, and a custom-built, three-story doll-house with "Dr. Ruth Westheimer, Sex Therapist" on the door. Someone said that Dr. Ruth's home was like a grandma's house crammed full of living.

Without a doubt, Dr. Westheimer enjoys the fruits of her success: the limousine, a well-known Fifth Avenue hairdresser, unbudgeted shopping, and the constant attention she receives wherever she goes. People stop her on the street and ask for her autograph. Cab drivers, construction workers, and policemen call out to her. And Dr. Ruth reacts like a little girl. She claps her hands and giggles. "I love it! I love it!" she cries.

But, in spite of a luxurious life, Dr. Ruth has not forgotten her professional obligations. She continues to lecture at universities and medical schools. She is an adjunct associate professor in the Human Sexuality Teaching Program at New York Hospital-Cornell Medical Center and a consultant in the division of Geriatric Medicine at New York University-Bellevue Hospital Medical Center. And she maintains a tiny office in downtown Manhattan where she has a private practice in psychotherapy. Her specialty is the treatment of sexual dysfunction. She is especially pleased to be a non-physician, honorary member of the New York Academy of

Dr. Ruth enjoys the fruits of her success. She loves to be recognized by fans and asked for her autograph.

Medicine. She writes scholarly papers and keeps up with sex education news by subscribing to journals and magazines and reading numerous books. Dr. Ruth speaks and reads fluently in German, French, Hebrew, and English.

In 1990, Dr. Ruth Westheimer was a cast member of *Dr. Ruth's House,* a television series considered by ABC. In this situation comedy, she portrayed a psychology professor who owns an off-campus rooming house. Her romantic interest in the series was a college dean. In filming the first episode, Dr. Ruth was supposed to kiss the dean. She admitted in a *Time* article that she thought she could fake the smooch. When she was asked to pucker up for the real thing, she said, "I was embarrassed. The whole world is going to watch me kiss. But I do like it." Her reaction to her film kiss is not surprising because enjoying whatever she is doing is part of her vibrant personality.

Dr. Ruth believes that coming to the United States was the best move she ever made. She remembers that first morning over thirty years ago. She had risen early that day. As the ship was entering the New York harbor, she saw the Statue of Liberty with the torch of freedom held high. She felt almost as if the Statue of Liberty was her personal welcome to the United States.

In 1986, Dr. Ruth Westheimer was asked to do a video for the one-hundredth anniversary celebration of the Statue of Liberty. This honor was special to Dr. Ruth, an immigrant, an exile. She had arrived in the United States with nothing but belief in her own potential, a positive, up-beat outlook on life, and hope in the future. America gave her freedom. She's worked hard and earned her superstar position, but she's the first to say, "What's happened to me could only have happened in America."

Further Reading

Books

Dolan, Edward F. *Adolf Hitler: A Portrait in Tyranny.* New York: Dodd, Mead & Company, 1981.

————. *Victory in Europe: The Fall of Hitler's Germany.* New York: Franklin Watts, 1988.

Gilbert, Martin. *The Second World War: A Complete History.* New York: Henry Holt & Company, 1989.

Shirer, William L. *The Rise & Fall of the Third Reich.* New York: Simon & Schuster, 1960.

Westheimer, Dr. Ruth. *All in a Lifetime.* New York: Warner Books, 1987.

Westheimer, Dr. Ruth and Kravetz, Dr. Nathan. *First Love: A Young People's Guide to Sexual Information.* New York: Warner Books, 1985.

Articles and Videos

Bosworth, Patricia. "Talking with Doctor Goodsex." *Ladies Home Journal,* February 1986.

Bruns, Bill, Emily Ormand and Alan Waldman. "It's Pilot Season, and High Concepts Are Circling Hollywood." *TV Guide,* March 10–16, 1990.

Dullea, Georgia. "Therapist to Therapist: Analyzing Dr. Ruth." *The New York Times,* October 26, 1987.

Dyckman, Constance. "The Fact of Love in the Library: Making Sexuality Information Relevant and Accessible to Young People." Videocassette, *School Library Journal,* April 1988.

Harrison, Barbara Grizzuti. "The Truth According to Dr. Ruth." *McCall's,* October 1983.

Jaynes, Gregory. "Over the Alps and Through the Shops with Dr. Ruth." *Life,* November 1987.

Mano, D. Keith, "The Gimlet Eye." *National Review,* May 13, 1983.

————. "Good Sex!" *People,* April 15, 1985.

"The Melody Lingers On." *People,* February 26, 1990.

Muck, Terry C. "A Sexpert's Ethics." *Christianity Today,* September 2, 1988.

"Oops." *People,* January 20, 1986.

Paley, Maggie. "Love, Sex, Romance & Dr. Ruth." *Vogue,* March 3, 1983.

"Pucker Up." *Time,* April 16, 1990.

Westheimer, Dr. Ruth. "Alive in My Heart." *Woman's Day,* December 22, 1987.

Westheimer, Dr. Ruth. "How I Would Improve Bugs' Love Life." *Time,* May 7, 1990.

Chronology

1928—Karola Ruth Siegel is born on June 4, in Frankfurt, Germany.

1938—Kristallnacht, "the night of the broken glass," occurs.

Karola's father is taken by the Nazis to the Buchenwald detention camp.

1939—World War II begins on September 1.

Karola is sent out of Germany as part of the Kinder Transport to Switzerland.

1941—Karola receives her last letter from her family.

1945—World War II ends on May 7.

Karola emigrates to Palestine and lives on a kibbutz.

Karola changes her name to Ruth K. Siegel.

1946—Ruth moves to another kibbutz in order to pursue an education.

1948—Ruth joins the Haganah, the Jewish underground army.

Israel becomes independent of British rule and is declared the Jewish homeland.

Israel enters war against the Arab league; Ruth is injured by an Arab bomb.

1949—The Arab-Israeli war ends.

Ruth receives her teaching certificate from a kindergarten seminary.

1950—Ruth marries David. The couple moves to Paris. Ruth studies at the Sorbonne to become a clinical psychologist.

1954—Ruth and David are divorced; David returns to Israel. Ruth falls in love with Dan.

1956—Ruth and Dan move to New York City and marry.

1957—Miriam, Ruth and Dan's daughter, is born.

1958—Dan and Ruth are divorced; Dan returns to Europe.

1959—Ruth graduates from the New School for Social Research with a master's degree in sociology.

1961—Ruth marries Fred Westheimer.

1964—Joel, Ruth and Fred's son, is born.

1965—Ruth becomes an American citizen.

1967—Ruth becomes project director for Planned Parenthood in Harlem.

1970—Ruth receives her Doctor of Education degree from Columbia University.

1972—Ruth receives her certificate in psychosexual therapy from Cornell Medical School.

1980—*Sexually Speaking*, Ruth's radio show, debuts on WYNY-FM.

1982—Ruth begins writing a monthly column for *Playgirl* magazine.

1983—*Dr. Ruth's Guide to Good Sex* is published.

1984—*Sexually Speaking* is syndicated by NBC.

Good Sex with Dr. Westheimer, Ruth's television show, airs; soon renamed *The Doctor Ruth Show*.

1985—*First Love: A Young People's Guide to Sexual Information* is published.

1986—*Dr. Ruth's Guide for Married Lovers* is published.

Ruth makes her acting debut in the film *One Woman Or Two*.

1987—*All in a Lifetime*, Ruth's autobiography, is published.

1990—Ruth appears in a TV pilot, *Dr. Ruth's House*, considered by ABC-TV.

Index

127

About the Author

Margaret M. Scariano is the author of numerous novels and non-fiction works for young people. She received her master's degree in English from Illinois State University and worked for many years as a teacher at Indian Valley Junior College. Ms. Scariano now devotes her time exclusively to writing. She and her husband, Franklin A. Scariano, live in California.